W9-BKX-727

THE PSYCHOLOGIST
AND THE FOREIGN-LANGUAGE
TEACHER

WILGA M. RIVERS

THE PSYCHOLOGIST
AND THE FOREIGN-LANGUAGE
TEACHER

THE UNIVERSITY OF CHICAGO PRESS
CHICAGO & LONDON

The University of Chicago Press, Chicago 60637
The University of Chicago Press, Ltd., London

© 1964 by The University of Chicago. All rights reserved
Published 1964. Printed in the United States of America

International Standard Book Number: 0-226-72095-0
Library of Congress Catalog Card Number: 64-15809

80 79 78 77 76   13 12 11 10 9

PREFACE

DURING the last quarter-century, theoretical psychology has found application in many fields, notably education and industry. Recently some psychologists have turned their attention specifically to the problems of language as a form of human behavior, while students of language, too, have sought deeper insights into the process of language acquisition. Foreign-language teachers in the schools are keenly interested in what scholars in both of these areas have to contribute to the improvement of work in the classroom or laboratory.

A clear-cut viewpoint on the teaching of foreign languages has emerged and is being increasingly adopted in the schools. The time has now come for a critical appraisal of this method, in the light of the most recent conclusions on the learning process. Such an appraisal should be of use to the classroom teacher as well as to the scholar and should lead to further improvement in instruction. This book was written with the classroom teacher in mind.

It is my hope that I have been able to clarify many areas of controversy for the teacher in the schools, helping him to draw from scholarly discussion ideas which will be of value to him in his relations with his students. Since I have had many years of experience in teaching foreign languages in high schools, it is also my hope that my conclusions may help the scholar to review theoretical assumptions from a practical perspective.

It is difficult to discuss coherently the special problems of three distinctly different age levels in one argument, and so I have concentrated on the teaching of foreign languages in high schools, because this is, and always will be, a vital part of the entire foreign-language program. Many of the conclusions will, however, apply to students at other levels of instruction, making due allowance for degree of maturity, emotional factors, and motivation.

In order to make the discussion more comprehensible to all who are interested and concerned, an appendix on psychological learning theory has been included. It is suggested that readers who are not familiar with learning theory, or who feel that their knowledge is outdated, should read this appendix after chapter III or use it for reference as they feel the need for further elucidation. The final chapter summarizes the many suggestions for the improvement of instruction which have emerged in the preceding chapters, without further reference to their psychological justification. This organization was decided on in the hope that the practical teacher may take away something of definite and immediate value from the reading of the book.

For continual help and encouragement in the extensive research that this study entailed, I particularly wish to thank Professors Harold Hand, Gilbert Kettelkamp, and R. Stewart Jones of the College of Education of the University of Illinois, and for their interest at all stages of its development, Professors Francis Nachtmann, Kenneth Henderson, and Lloyd McCleary. I am also grateful to Professor O. Hobart Mowrer for his critical reading of the chapter on conditioning, to Professor Morris Freilich for providing reference material in the area of anthropological linguistics, and to Jean Praninskas for allowing free and frequent access to her personal library and for her generous assistance in the reading of the proofs.

DeKalb, Illinois

CONTENTS

I

INTRODUCTION

THERE are now 80,000 foreign students in the United States; 110 nations have representatives in New York at the United Nations; about 100,000 American students spend the summer in Europe, Asia, Africa, and Latin America;[1] the Peace Corps aimed at having nine thousand members in forty-two countries by September, 1963:[2] aid programs send technicians and specialists to all corners of the globe; and travel agencies send tourists to increasingly far-flung vacation spots. Millions of Americans are hearing the strange tones and rhythms of other languages and are becoming fascinated by the possibility of learning to communicate with people in their own tongues.

"Learning to speak a foreign language now comes easily, naturally—faster than ever before," says an advertisement in the *New Yorker*. "15 minutes a day with an 'Instant' Language Record Set—in the relaxed surroundings of his home or office—and the man you singled out for this thoughtful gift will be speaking French, Spanish, Russian, Italian or German within 10 days. By the time he completes the course, he will have a speaking vocabulary of more than 3500 words and 1000 phrases. He will use authentic native pronunciation, and will be able to carry on a conversation with astonishing ease." What is the secret of this new "in-

---

[1] Dr. Benjamin Fine, "U. S. Students Hit the Road," *Champaign-Urbana Courier*, July 17, 1962, p. 19.

[2] J. Landgraf, "Peace Corps and Languages," *The Linguistic Reporter*, II (April, 1963), p. 1.

stant" success? "Reinforced Learning is a modern, scientific method based on principles developed by famous educators at Harvard and Columbia universities. Thoroughly tested and proved by the armed services, and successfully used by private industry in training and personnel up-grading programs, this method is now available for home language study through 'Instant' Language Records." At last our modern scientific knowledge, having already produced miracle drugs and electronic computers, seems to have succeeded in shortening the long, long road of language mastery. What the advertisement does not mention is that those army courses involve some nine hours a day of intensive study for as long as nine months, in what can hardly be called "relaxed surroundings."

If we ourselves are too lazy to learn a new language, even by this modern miracle method, why not give our children the chance to learn the painless way? "Since there is no known limit to the number of languages a small child can learn in a natural cultural setting," says Theodore Andersson, "one might start [in an international nursery school] with as many languages as there are days in the week. For practical purposes I should select Chinese, French, German, Russian and Spanish . . . . On Monday the Spanish-speaking teacher would be in charge and would conduct her work in Spanish. On Tuesday the Russian teacher would direct the activities in Russian. On Wednesday the German teacher would take over, as would the Chinese teacher on Thursday and the French teacher on Friday . . . . It is my guess . . . that the children would understand everything that is said in this limited setting in all five languages by the end of the school year."[3]

Such is the interest in foreign languages throughout the community that there is at present no lack of money for foreign-language projects. High schools are establishing programs or lengthening those already established;[4] elemen-

---

[3] "After FLES [Foreign Languages in the Elementary School]—What?" *Educational Forum*, XXVI, No. 1 (November, 1961), 84–85.

[4] Four-year courses in high schools were strongly recommended by J. B. Conant in his report on *The American High School Today* (New York, 1959), pp. 69–73.

tary schools are joining in the national effort; language laboratories are being installed; new materials appear as fast as they can be printed or taped. As William Riley Parker says in the third edition of *The National Interest and Foreign Languages*, released by the Department of State in March, 1962, there is no longer any need to promote the cause of foreign languages: "Public interest is high; it has already made itself effective through the Congress of the United States; it needs, hereafter, to be better informed about the complexities of the language problem."[5]

The present revival of interest in the teaching of foreign languages in the schools of the United States does not, according to Parker, date from Sputnik I. "Even language teachers do not yet realize," he says, "that the Language Development Program (Title VI) of the National Defense Education Act was fully formulated before any Sputnik rocketed our linguistic weaknesses into new prominence."[6] Since 1952, the teachers of modern foreign languages in the United States have been working together, under the aegis of the Modern Language Association, to improve foreign-language instruction. They have been greatly influenced in their recommendations by the work of the linguistic scientists[7] and the methods developed under their guidance in the army and Foreign Service programs, and in such well-known university programs as those of Cornell, Georgetown, Michigan, and California (UCLA).[8]

Parallel to this surge of interest in methods of teaching which are consistent with a particular theory of the nature of language has come increasing research in the psychology of language, or psycholinguistics. These two trends have converged as a result of the growing emphasis on inter-

---

[5] William Riley Parker, *The National Interest and Foreign Languages*, discussion guide prepared for the U. S. National Commission for UNESCO (Washington, D. C., 1962), p. 9.

[6] *Ibid.*, p. 8.

[7] This term will be used when referring to the scholars who adopt the descriptive approach to language of the Linguistic Society of America. For a full account of the development of American linguistics, see J. B. Carroll, *The Study of Language* (Cambridge, Mass., 1953), chap. ii.

[8] *Ibid.*, pp. 170–83, gives a detailed account of developments from 1941 to 1953.

disciplinary research, and seminars have brought together linguistic scientists, psychologists, and foreign-language teachers. As a result of this growing interest in the psychology of language, recent books on the theory and practice of foreign-language teaching have found place for some reference to the subject. These discussions of the psychology upon which teaching methods are based are mostly rather brief, but the consensus seems to be that "the linguistic method conforms with the most recent theories on the psychology of learning."[9] This idea has gradually permeated foreign-language teaching circles and reached the wider public; hence the appeal of the advertisement quoted earlier.

Serious study of the contribution that the psychology of learning can make to the improvement of foreign-language teaching is of fairly recent date, however. Since H. R. Huse published his book on *The Psychology of Foreign Language Study* in 1931, there has been no comparable study relating the research of psychological learning theory to the special problems of foreign-language teaching. In 1948, H. B. Dunkel devoted thirteen pages of his book on *Second-Language Learning* to "The Language-Learning of the Child— the Processes and the Types of Learning Involved," relating his conclusions to foreign-language learning.[10] In *The Study of Language* (1953), J. B. Carroll devoted only one page to the psychology of learning foreign languages,[11] although he gave fairly detailed accounts of the history of interest in linguistic problems in psychology and of the nature of language behavior in the native speaker. In *Language and Language Learning, Theory and Practice* (1960), Nelson Brooks discussed the nature of language, the way the child learns his native language, and bilingualism. He devoted three pages to types and theories of learning[12] but did

---

[9] S. Simches and J. Bruno, "A Psycholinguistic Rationale for FLES," *Tufts University Interdisciplinary Research Seminar on Psycholinguistics and Foreign Language Teaching*, 1961, p. 2.

[10] H. B. Dunkel, *Second-Language Learning* (Boston, 1948), pp. 14–26.

[11] Carroll (1953), p. 99.

[12] N. Brooks, *Language and Language Learning, Theory and Practice* (New York, 1960), chap. iv.

not pursue the subject of their possible application to the classroom situation, although he referred from time to time to the concept of reinforcement without further elucidating it.[13]

In November, 1960, J. B. Carroll prepared a very complete account of the "Research on Teaching of Foreign Languages" up to that date, discussing all the experiments relevant to specific areas of foreign-language study and making a number of recommendations about outstanding problems that warrant research.[14]

In the report prepared in 1961 for the Ninth International Congress of Linguists, *Trends in European and American Linguistics*, William Moulton wrote a very interesting and well-documented account of "Linguistics and Language Teaching in the United States 1940-1960."[15] In this article he outlined the "linguistic principles" on which the new language teaching is based. These principles, he stated, are that "Language is speech, not writing. . . . A language is a set of habits. . . . Teach the language, not about the language. . . . A language is what its native speakers say, not what someone thinks they ought to say. . . . Languages are different." He called these "the slogans of the day." Moulton did not, however, mention research into the psychology of foreign-language learning.

During the same year, other writers paid more detailed attention to what psychological learning theory can contribute to foreign-language teaching. Robert Politzer devoted a chapter in both *Teaching French: An Introduction to Applied Linguistics* and *Teaching Spanish: A Linguistic Orientation* to "Some Psychological Aspects of Language

---

[13] George Miller's very thorough study of *Language and Communication* (1951) gives much excellent material on the perception of speech and verbal behavior, but he is concerned with the learning of native, not foreign, language. *Words and Things* (1958), by Roger Brown, gives a thorough analysis of many aspects of the psychology of language, including the "Original Word Game" of learning the native language, but does not mention foreign-language learning.

[14] J. B. Carroll (Harvard, 1960; mimeographed), prepared for the *Handbook of Research on Teaching* (Rand McNally & Co., 1963).

[15] C. Mohrmann, A. Sommerfelt, and J. Whatmough (eds.), *Trends in European and American Linguistics 1930–1960* (Utrecht, 1961), pp. 82–109.

Learning,"[16] and, in the summer of 1961, the Tufts University Interdisciplinary Research Seminar on Psycholinguistics and Foreign Language Teaching published a report containing eight papers by linguistic scientists, psychologists, and foreign-language teachers, on such subjects as "A Psycholinguistic Rationale for FLES," "Learning Theory, Language Development and Language Learning," "Ontogenetic Development of Language," "Semantic and Syntactic Development," and "Psychometrics in Second Language Learning."[17]

Interest in this subject is growing rapidly, and further useful areas of psychological learning theory are gradually being investigated. In September, 1962, Wallace Lambert presented a paper to the Seminar of Language Teacher Training at the University of Washington on "Psychological Approaches to the Study of Language,"[18] and he and his associates at McGill University in Montreal, Quebec, are engaged in a number of valuable experiments in this area. Other experiments are in progress in many centers in the United States under contract with the Office of Education Language Development Program,[19] and, where appropriate, reports of those already completed have been used in this study.

This book endeavors to make a contribution to this area of mounting interest, specifically by applying the findings of psychological learning theory to the assumptions which are basic to certain techniques at present employed in many schools. A specific approach to foreign-language teaching has emerged, of recent years, from the association of lin-

---

[16] Both of these books by Politzer were published by Ginn & Co., Boston, in 1961.

[17] Tufts University (1961), OE Contract SAE-9494 for the Language Development Program of the U. S. Office of Education.

[18] This paper by Wallace Lambert has been made available to foreign-language teachers in the *Modern Language Journal*, XLVII, No. 2 (February, 1963), 51–62, and No. 3 (March, 1963), 114–21.

[19] A complete list of these, with contractors, will be found in *Language Development Program: Research and Studies*, OE 12011 for the first two years, OS 12011-61 for 1961, and OE 12014-62 for 1962. *Completed Research, Studies, and Instructional Materials, List No. 2*, OE 12016, indicates materials produced to the end of 1962 under this program (Washington, D. C., U. S. Office of Education).

guistic scientists and foreign-language teachers. This approach, usually called the audio-lingual method, purports to be soundly based on psychological theory. As it becomes more and more widely accepted by foreign-language teachers and as new textbooks, language laboratory materials, articles in professional journals, and books on method take its tenets as beyond dispute, teachers should know to what extent its claims to be based on experimentally attested psychological principles are legitimate.

To this end, an examination will be made of the theory behind the audio-lingual method and its major assumptions about the foreign-language learning process. These will then be examined in the light of psychological learning theory. Those aspects of learning theory that have been experimentally tested and validated will be taken as authoritative for the purposes of this study, which will not attempt to adjudicate differences between learning theorists. In this way, the research of psychologists will be used to show whether these major assumptions are basic to the foreign-language learning process as such or are merely assumptions about a particular method of teaching a foreign language. Where criticism seems warranted in the light of the psychological findings cited, recommendations will be made for the improvement of the techniques under discussion.

As the experience of the writer has been in the teaching of French, examples will be drawn from this language. That the same methods are being advocated, however, for other modern foreign languages is demonstrated by the fact that the publishers of the Audio-Lingual Materials (A-L M) print the same introductory section on methods in the *Teacher's Manual* for each of the modern foreign languages for which they provide materials. The conclusions of this study are therefore intended to apply equally to the teaching of other foreign languages. The application of theory to classroom practice will further be limited to the problems of teaching a foreign language to students of high school age, as the problems of elementary school and college students are in many ways not comparable to those of high school students. Much of what is said will, undoubtedly, be found to apply at other levels, when due attention has been paid to differences in educational development, emotional factors, and motivation.

No attempt will be made to discuss priority of objectives and expected outcomes in foreign-language learning, because the writer does not consider that they derive from the nature of language and of the foreign-language learning process; they are considered rather to be preferences established according to geographical, historical, or contemporary exigencies and not examinable in relation to psychological learning theory. In *Learning Theory and Behavior*, Mowrer states as his considered opinion that learning theory "has little or nothing to say about what living organisms, and human beings in particular, *ought* to learn or what in fact they *do* learn: yet this is a question with which parents, teachers, ministers, jurists and many others are deeply concerned. Learning theory may help such persons, once they have decided upon their objectives, to attain them; but it never, or at least only rarely, dictates what these objectives should be."[20] There may well be reasons why some particular individual may wish to learn to read a foreign language but not to write or speak it. Another individual may wish to learn to understand it when spoken but not to read it. These decisions are based on personal requirements but, once they are made, an understanding of learning processes may help these individuals to attain their objectives. Understanding of learning processes may show that a student learns to read a foreign language better if he speaks it first, but this is another question and does not change his established priority of objectives.

Before we can settle down to any fruitful discussion of the psychological warranty of the audio-lingual method, it will be necessary to describe the method in detail, as it is advocated in certain well-known and widely read publications. The major assumptions of psychological import to be considered will be drawn from this description. These assumptions will be listed with accompanying quotations from the sources chosen, as evidence that they are in fact explicit and implicit in the statements of these writers. In

---

[20] O. Hobart Mowrer, *Learning Theory and Behavior* (New York, 1960), p. 7.

subsequent chapters, these major assumptions, with certain corollaries, will be examined in detail in the light of psychological learning theory and experimental research. Finally, the psychological findings and methodological recommendations will be summarized for easy reference and practical application.

II

THE AUDIO-LINGUAL METHOD DESCRIBED

ANYONE reading professional journals in the foreign-language teaching field recently must have become aware of something controversial stirring the teachers. A large number of articles are appearing on new methods that are unfamiliar to many teachers. Books on teaching methods and new materials all seem to sound the same note: this is the new key, this is the scientific way of teaching a foreign language. "The linguist . . . has made important discoveries concerning the psychological processes involved in language learning."[1] One turns the page and there finds other teachers expressing very strong reactions to forceful advocacy of the new key. Virginia Cables, of La Habra High School in California, asks "Have you been 'rushed'?" Her feeling is that "though still nameless, the society for the propagation of the 'oral method' for the teaching of foreign languages has been 'rushing' prospective members, much as other fraternal societies do," and she goes on to recount her experiences after she "pledged."[2] Vincenzo Cioffari speaks of "small groups enthused with a missionary zeal" who "have come to feel that they alone have the secret formula for bringing about improvement in the profession."[3]

---

[1] J. Bruno and S. Simches, "A Psycholinguistic Rationale for FLES," *French Review*, XXXV (May, 1962), 583.

[2] "Pre-reading vs. Post-reading," *Modern Language Journal*, XLV (October, 1961), 252.

[3] "The Influence of the Language Institute Program—Past, Present, and Future," *Modern Language Journal*, XLVI (February, 1962), 65.

Edward Heise of the U.S. Naval Academy particularly objects to official support for a given method by professional associations. In an article entitled "Let's Talk Sense about Language Teaching," he says, "Are we going to find ourselves in the position where our professional organizations become partisans of an 'official dogma' and all non-conformists 'heretics'? Is it possible that our professional group can become so deeply committed to one school of thought that the doctrine must be defended to avoid losing face? . . . Already many articles reflect a tendency to offer quotations from the new 'authorities' as conclusive demonstration of a controversial point. Already there is an inclination to see things in the extremes of 'good' or 'bad.' "[4] Brooks, who is a leading exponent of the audio-lingual method, maintains on the other hand that "no single method is preferred. Many different methods are found to be effective, with this important proviso—objectives must remain constant. A method that inhibits the student's advance by encouraging wrong learning cannot be recommended."[5] As objectives provide the controversial element which largely determines methods, and as "wrong learning" in this context must mean "learning which does not achieve the objectives we consider the most important," Brooks' statement does not reassure teachers like those just quoted.

It would seem important to know exactly what are the essential features of this "program of language learning for communication" which Brooks says "is based upon broad professional agreement about objectives, methods, materials, tests, and outcomes."[6] These features are set out specifically in several sources, among them the statement of the Modern Language Association, "FL Program Policy"

[4] *The French Review*, XXXV (December, 1961), 176.
[5] S. L. Flaxman (ed.), *Modern Language Teaching in School and College*, Northeast Conference on the Teaching of Foreign Languages, 1961, Reports of the Working Committees (Princeton, 1961), p. 15 [hereinafter referred to as Northeast Conference (1961)]. The Foreword by Brooks and the Report of Working Committee III ("The Transition to the Classroom"), were reprinted in *The Teacher's Notebook in Modern Foreign Languages*, Fall, 1961, issued by Harcourt, Brace & World, Inc., School Department, and sent out with the Audio-Lingual Materials (A-L M).
[6] Northeast Conference (1961), p. 17.

(*PMLA*, September, 1956, Part II); *Modern Foreign Languages and the Academically Talented Student* (NEA, 1960); Nelson Brooks, *Language and Language Learning, Theory and Practice* (New York, 1960); Robert Politzer, *Teaching French: An Introduction to Applied Linguistics* (Boston, 1961); *Modern Language Teaching in School and College*, edited by S. L. Flaxman, containing the reports of the Working Committees to the 1961 Northeast Conference on the Teaching of Foreign Languages (Princeton, 1961); and the *Teacher's Manual*, prepared by the staff of the Modern Language Materials Development Center (New York, 1961), to accompany the Audio-Lingual Materials (A-L M) for French Level One. An analysis of these sources shows a remarkable degree of concurrence, indicating that the leaders of the audio-lingual movement have a very clear idea of the objectives, principles, and procedures which they jointly advocate.

"The learning of a modern foreign language," says Brooks, "is a single discipline with its own objectives and learning procedures, its own characteristic content and expected outcomes."[7] The objectives are understood in all these sources to be "proficiency in language skills accompanied by familiarity with the outstanding traits of the foreign culture,"[8] the language skills being the four listed on the trademark of the Audio-Lingual Materials: listening, speaking, reading, and writing. These four skills must be learned "in that order," as Brooks puts it, or "in their proper order," as Working Committee III of the Northeast Conference on the Teaching of Foreign Languages states even more categorically.[9] "The student should understand the foreign language as it is spoken by native speakers in situations similar to his own experience . . . . He should speak the foreign language in everyday situations with reasonable fluency and correctness, and with pronunciation acceptable to the native speaker of the language . . . . He

---

[7] *Teacher's Manual* (1961), p. 2.

[8] W. Starr, M. Thompson, and D. Walsh (eds.), *Modern Foreign Languages and the Academically Talented Student* (New York, N.E.A., 1960), p. 9 [hereinafter referred to as NEA (1960)].

[9] Northeast Conference (1961), p. 43.

should read the foreign language easily and without conscious translation . . . . He should be able to communicate in writing anything he can say . . . . Mastery of the skills must be accompanied by familiarity with the culture the language represents, as well as a larger view of life resulting from the realization that there are many cultures and value systems, some far different from our own, operative in the world today."[10] The literary objective is not ignored, but it is considered to be implicit in the others. "Since language is the chief element of which literature is made, the development of language competence cannot fail to strengthen the understanding of literature. In suitable proportions, selected samples of good literature are important in language programs from the beginning."[11]

In "Research on Teaching Foreign Languages," prepared for the *Handbook of Research on Teaching* (November, 1960), Carroll lists four essential characteristics of "the method of foreign language teaching towards which there seems now to be convergence." They are, briefly, as follows (pages 8–10):

1. Items are normally presented and learned in their spoken form before they are presented in their written form.

2. Teaching methods rest upon the careful scientific analysis of the contrasts between the learner's language and the target language.

3. Stress is laid on the need for overlearning of language patterns by a special type of drill known as "pattern practice."

4. There is an insistence on the desirability, or even the necessity, of learning to make responses in situations which simulate "real-life" communication situations as closely as possible.

As the writer's own research has shown these to be very useful categories for a more detailed analysis of the distinctive features of the audio-lingual method, they will be used as a general framework.

1. *Items presented in spoken form before written form.*

---

[10] NEA (1960), pp. 17–19.
[11] Northeast Conference (1961), p. 18.

It is from this first principle that the method has derived
the name *audio-lingual*. "Language is primarily what is
said and only secondarily what is written."[12] "The first or
audio-lingual stage is by far the most important; . . . it
lays an indispensable foundation for the other two (reading
and writing). In this first stage, only the ear and tongue
are trained, without use of the written language."[13]

Various derivative emphases are made in all the sources:
Accurate pronunciation should be developed, with native
phonology, structures and intonation, and with mastery
of the sound system before the spelling system. To insure
such mastery, an adequate model to imitate is essential
(teacher or native informant), and for older students a
clear description of the sound system is useful. This order,
spoken form before written form, is considered to be the
natural order, as it was the order in which the mother
tongue was learned. Consequently, in the early stages of
reading students will read only what they have already
learned to understand and to say. "How soon students
reach the stage of safe initial exposure to written material
will depend on their age, their language skill, and the
language they are learning."[14] In this way they will be
able to read directly in the foreign language from the
beginning.

2. *Careful scientific analysis of contrasts between the
learner's language and the target language.* This is of
course the distinctive contribution of the linguistic scientists, and the results of studies of these contrasts are incorporated in the materials prepared for class and language
laboratory work.[15]

3. *Need for overlearning of language patterns by a
special type of drill known as "pattern practice."* Basic
to this principle is a belief about what language is and a
theory of learning. Brooks says, "Language is learned,
systematic, symbolic vocal behavior; a culturally acquired,

---

[12] Brooks (1960), p. 20.
[13] NEA (1960), p. 20.
[14] *Ibid.*, p. 23.
[15] See, for example, the *Contrastive Structure Series*, ed. Charles A.
Ferguson, published by the University of Chicago Press.

universal, and exclusive mark of man."[16] Politzer continues, "Language is 'behavior' and . . . behavior can be learned only by inducing the student to 'behave'—in other words to perform in the language."[17] *"The single paramount fact about language learning,"* Brooks insists, *"is that it concerns, not problem-solving, but the formation and performance of habits."*[18] "Increment learning is particularly significant. One does not learn by making mistakes, but rather by giving the right response," he says elsewhere,[19] while Politzer adds: "Correct responses are learned better if they are immediately reinforced by reward."[20]

The method advocated for the development of these language habits is that of "pattern practice" or "structure drill" which, Brooks says, "makes no pretense of being communication. . . . It is . . . exercise in structural dexterity undertaken solely for the sake of practice, in order that performance may become habitual and automatic."[21] Clear instructions on how to conduct such pattern practice are given in each of the sources.[22] The teacher presents a typical structure in the foreign language, drills the student in correct pronunciation and intonation, and then uses it as a "frame" for modeling other utterances by such processes as substitution, expansion, and transformation.[23] Each change made is minimal, and this practice continues to the point of saturation or automatic performance. As Politzer says, "Linguistically oriented materials are thus apt to form a continuum of drills and exercises."[24]

It is not surprising therefore that advocates of the audio-lingual method have been enthusiastic supporters of the

---

[16] *Teacher's Manual* (1961), p. 2.

[17] Politzer (1961), p. 2.

[18] Brooks (1960), p. 47.

[19] *Teacher's Manual* (1961), p. 3.

[20] Politzer (1961), p. 32.

[21] Brooks (1960), p. 142.

[22] Except the Modern Language Association's "FL Program Policy" (1956), which is concerned with objectives and principles, not procedures.

[23] Politzer (1961), pp. 23–26; E. Stack, *The Language Laboratory and Modern Language Teaching* (New York, 1960), pp. 7–31.

[24] Politzer (1961), p. 29.

language laboratory as a powerful aid in the automatization of language responses. Electronic equipment is unwearying in its presentation of drill material with minimal changes, and responses can be corrected or rewarded immediately as the machine presents the correct version.

Grammar is thus presented first through the drilling of structures, after which a simple "generalization" may be made about the grammatical principle involved. This generalization then describes what the student is doing, instead of prescribing what he ought to do.[25] As the audio-lingual method does not proscribe the use of the native language in the classroom (although strictly limiting its use to the teacher), this explanation may be made in the native language.

4. *Learning to make responses in situations which simulate "real-life" communication situations as closely as possible.* "The study of a foreign language . . . is a progressive *experience*" as well as the "progressive acquisition of a *skill* . . . enlarging the pupil's horizon through the introduction to a new medium of communication and a new culture pattern."[26] In the audio-lingual system, these two aspects of language-learning are combined in the dialogue method of instruction, in which new structures are carefully introduced and practiced in a matrix of allusions to another way of life and a different set of values. As Brooks says pertinently, "When language is in action, there is always a speaker. He is always somewhere, speaking to someone, about something. *Unless the facts of persons and places are taken into account as well as linguistic facts, we do not have the full dimension of language.*"[27] And Politzer agrees: "Unless we understand the cultural situation in which an utterance is made, we may miss its full implication or meaning."[28]

The method of teaching such dialogues is also set out

---

[25] *Ibid.*, p. 11.
[26] "Values of Foreign Language Study" in M.L.A., "FL Program Policy" (1956).
[27] Brooks (1960), p. 106.
[28] Politzer (1961), p. 130.

in considerable detail in the sources.[29] The dialogue should be "overlearned" to the point of automatic response to the dialogue situation, practiced in various adaptations, and used again in "directed dialogue." This is quite obviously a similar approach to that advocated for pattern practice, but this time with connected situational material, thus drawing nearer to "the ultimate objective . . . the free use of the foreign language in meaningful conversation within the limits of the student's control of structure and vocabulary."[30]

Naturally, reading materials are not neglected in this method. After students have been carefully introduced to reading, it is urged that there should be provision for much reading of authentic material. Such material should be graded in linguistic difficulty and suited to the maturity of the student, so that he may from the beginning read directly in the foreign language without deciphering or translation. Thus, the literary objective may be pursued side by side with the cultural and linguistic objectives, but oral practice must always be kept to the fore by conducting all discussion of reading materials in the foreign language.

It may be noted that the building of an extensive vocabulary has not been mentioned. The consensus in the sources is that this should be subordinated to a sound foundational knowledge of structure, by which words, when learned later, can be fitted correctly into discourse. All vocabulary should be learned in context, and word-lists pairing foreign-language words with "equivalents" in the native language should not be used for teaching purposes. Thus, enlarging of the student's vocabulary takes place at the later reading stage.

Writing the foreign language, according to the sources, should be introduced gradually and should keep strictly to what the student has heard and repeated. Eventually he should be able to write anything he can say, draw up a simple report or summary, and write descriptions and letters. Fine translation is, however, a difficult art which

---

[29] Northeast Conference (1961), pp. 43–44; NEA (1960), p. 21; Brooks (1960), p. 141; *Teacher's Manual* (1961), p. 11.
[30] NEA (1960), p. 23.

should be left to the advanced stages of language study, when a high standard of work should be demanded.

Many features of the audio-lingual method which have been outlined will have a familiar ring to experienced teachers of foreign languages. As Carroll has said: "The emphasis on modern linguistic analysis and upon large amounts of drill on graded materials (represent) new departures, but only in degree. But then, in these highly advanced times it could hardly be expected that a new method would represent anything more than a new combination of procedures."[31] It is interesting to note that the most controversial elements, and those most forcefully advocated, apply to the earlier stages of language-learning. Experiments have not yet shown whether these have a decisive long-range effect on the final outcome of a reasonably long period of learning one foreign language.

---

[31] Carroll (1953), p. 177.

III

MAJOR ASSUMPTIONS
ABOUT LANGUAGE LEARNING
OF THE AUDIO-LINGUAL METHOD

THERE ARE four basic assumptions to be listed. The first is an inclusive statement, with certain minor assumptions which follow from the psychological position taken. These will be dealt with as corollaries of the main statement and will be examined individually.

ASSUMPTION 1. FOREIGN-LANGUAGE LEARNING IS BASICALLY A MECHANICAL[1] PROCESS OF HABIT FORMATION. Quotations from the sources follow:

> There is probably no general cure for the type of interference that comes from clinging to intellectual understanding in favor of automatic responses.[2]

> The single paramount fact about language learning is that it concerns not problem-solving but the formation and performance of habits.[3]

---

[1] "Mechanical" is used here in the sense of Brownell's "arbitrary association." It is intended to distinguish the process from an intellectual or emotional one. Politzer (1961) writes of "several months of uninterrupted pattern drills and mechanical stimulus response manipulations" (p. 19). Agard and Dunkel (1948), when investigating the oral-aural methods, said, "The cardinal principle was that the acquisition of oral and aural ability, in a second as in the first language, is primarily a mechanical rather than an intellectual process, comparable to a skill in art or craft and not to a mental discipline" (p. 281). "Oral-aural" was later replaced by "audio-lingual" as the name for these methods.

[2] Politzer (1961), p. 17.

[3] Brooks (1960), p. 47.

During [the drilling] period ask the students to focus their attention *solely on the changes in sound.*[4]

Drill . . . [speech patterns] by various techniques until the student has them under complete and automatic control. Once this control is achieved, a simple statement of the grammatical principle involved may be made.[5]

In addition to intellectual effort, language requires the automatic performance of a series of complex motor skills. These can be acquired only by saturation practice.[6]

The process is a type of learning that involves the establishment of a set of habits that are both neural and muscular, and that must be so well learned that they function automatically.[7]

The other possibility . . . that has been proved feasible . . . is to eliminate meaning almost totally from the initial phase of language instruction. It is entirely possible to teach the major patterns of a foreign language without letting the student know what he is saying . . . . Only *after* the student has gained complete and automatic control over the grammatical patterns would he be acquainted with the precise meaning of what he has learned.[8]

Corollary 1: *Habits are strengthened by reinforcement.*[9]

Corollary 2: *Foreign-language habits are formed most effectively by giving the right response, not by making mistakes.*[10]

Corollary 3: *"Language is 'behavior' and . . . behavior can be learned only by inducing the student to 'behave.'"*[11]

---

[4] *Teacher's Manual* (1961), p. 25.

[5] NEA (1960), p. 21.

[6] Northeast Conference (1961), p. 44.

[7] Brooks (1960), p. 21.

[8] Politzer (1961), p. 19; but Politzer adds, "Its general applicability at various levels of teaching remains to be studied."

[9] *Ibid.*, p. 32; Brooks (1960), p. 139.

[10] *Teacher's Manual* (1961), p. 3; Politzer (1961), p. 14.

[11] Politzer (1961), p. 2.

ASSUMPTION 2. LANGUAGE SKILLS ARE LEARNED MORE EFFEC-
TIVELY IF ITEMS OF THE FOREIGN LANGUAGE ARE PRESENTED IN
SPOKEN FORM BEFORE WRITTEN FORM. Quotations from the
sources follow:

> [The teacher] will present the four skills in their
> proper order (hearing, speaking, reading, writ-
> ing). The student will learn to understand what he
> hears the teacher speak, he will speak what he has
> heard modeled correctly, he will read what he has
> spoken, and he will write what he has spoken and
> read.[12]

> The first or audio-lingual stage is by far the most
> important . . . ; it lays an indispensable foundation
> for the other two (reading and writing). In the
> first stage, only the ear and tongue are trained,
> without use of the written language.[13]

> The learning of comprehension and speaking should in its
> initial stage be completely disassociated from the learning
> of reading and writing.[14]

> Language is something you understand and say
> *before* it is something you read and write. This
> principle should be applied not only at the begin-
> ning but also at later levels.[15]

ASSUMPTION 3. ANALOGY PROVIDES A BETTER FOUNDATION
FOR FOREIGN-LANGUAGE LEARNING THAN ANALYSIS. Quotations
from the sources follow:

> The learner who has only been made to see how
> language works has not learned any language; *on
> the contrary he has learned something he will have
> to forget* before he can make any progress in that
> area of language.[16]

> If drills have been sufficiently representative and
> have been practiced, analogy will guide the learner

---

12 Northeast Conference (1961), p. 43.
13 NEA (1960), p. 20.
14 Politzer (1961), p. 69.
15 Northeast Conference (1961), p. 18.
16 Brooks (1961), p. 47.

along the right linguistic path, as it does in the mother tongue.[17]

More importance is given to analogy and less to analysis until a considerable body of language materials has been learned.[18]

[What the student needs] is a perception of the analogies involved, of the structural differences, and similarities between sentences.[19]

ASSUMPTION 4. THE MEANINGS WHICH THE WORDS OF A LANGUAGE HAVE FOR THE NATIVE SPEAKER CAN BE LEARNED ONLY IN A MATRIX OF ALLUSIONS TO THE CULTURE OF THE PEOPLE WHO SPEAK THAT LANGUAGE. Quotations from the sources follow:

Unless we understand the cultural situation in which an utterance is made, we may miss its full implication or meaning. The tie of language study with culture is not an "option" to be discussed in terms of the preferences of the individual teacher, but actually a practical necessity.[20]

The student should come to realize that language is the essential expression of a people's behavior and outlook, the medium in which and by which they think about and react to life . . . . The student should acquire understanding and appreciation of another people's way of life, institutions, literature, and civilization.[21]

Without understanding of that culture, the meaning of words can never be understood.[22]

If we teach language without teaching at the same time the culture in which it operates, we are teaching meaningless symbols or symbols to which the student attaches the wrong meaning.[23]

---

[17] *Ibid.*, p. 139.
[18] *Teacher's Manual* (1961), p. 3.
[19] Politzer (1961), p. 15.
[20] *Ibid.*, p. 130.
[21] NEA (1960), pp. 19–20.
[22] *Teacher's Manual* (1961), p. 3.
[23] Politzer, "Report of the Fifth Annual Round Table Meeting on Linguistics and Language Teaching," pp. 100–101, as quoted in Brooks (1960), p. 86.

IV

SOME VIEWPOINTS ON WHAT LANGUAGE IS

BEFORE any decision can be made about the best way of teaching a language, it is well to consider what language is. This appears to be a simple enough question, but unfortunately students of language do not agree. There is a tremendous diversity of opinion.

At one extreme is the quasi-mystical viewpoint of Ruth Anshen, that "words are incarnations of ideas," that "there is present under the substructure of the formal diversity of the symbol a hidden essence which contains an essential and universal identity . . . . Language exists *ab aeterno,* immutable in its transcendant purity and revealing itself from time to time in the historical existence of mankind."[1]

This attitude is in vivid contrast to the severely abstract idea of language held by many linguistic scientists engaged in structural analysis, of whom Joos may be taken as an example. To Joos, language is "a symbolic communication system, or in one word . . . a 'code,'" which is essentially telegraphic. This code uses "molecular signals made up of invariant atoms." It has "numerous layers of complexity . . . and in each layer there are severe limitations upon the combinations permitted."[2] It is this abstract idea of language, completely detached from personality, social situa-

---

[1] Ruth Nanda Anshen, *Language: An Enquiry into Its Meaning and Function* ("Science of Culture Series," Vol. VIII [New York, 1957]), chap. i.

[2] M. Joos, "Description of Language Design," *Readings in Linguistics* (New York, 1958), pp. 353, 356.

tion, or the immutable idea of Anshen, which has enabled linguistic scientists to describe language structure purely in terms of the distribution and interrelationships of linguistic items.

The word "communication," however, presupposes a speaker and a hearer, and these cannot be ignored. To Bloomfield, language is "the rigid system of patterns of contrastive features through which the individual speech acts of a speaker become effective substitute stimuli (signals) for a hearer. With this rigid system of patterns we *can predict* the regular responses of the members of a linguistic community, when they are effectively stimulated by one of the patterns of the system."[3] The "individual speech acts" are what de Saussure has called "parole," to be distinguished carefully from "langue," the social side of speech which the individual can never create or modify by himself but must learn in its conventional form.[4]

This conventional form contains distinctive elements in each culture, and Trager brings this aspect into his definition of language as "a system of arbitrary vocal symbols by means of which the members of a society interact in terms of their total culture."[5]

Moving over to the field of psychology, we find that B. F. Skinner has taken up the question of language as a form of human behavior. The aspect of language on which he concentrates is that which linguists call "parole," that is, the individual's use of conventional speech patterns. This he calls "verbal behavior," and he seeks to account for its dynamic characteristics "within a framework appropriate to human behavior as a whole."[6] "We have no reason to assume," he says, ". . . that verbal behavior differs in any fundamental respect from non-verbal behavior, or that any new principles must be invoked to account for

[3] C. C. Fries, "The 'Bloomfield School,' " *Trends* (1961), p. 221.

[4] F. de Saussure, *Course in General Linguistics* (New York, 1959), p. 14.

[5] G. L. Trager, "The Field of Linguistics" ("S. I. L. Occasional Papers," Vol. I [Oklahoma City, 1949]), p. 4.

[6] B. F. Skinner, *Verbal Behavior* (New York, 1957), p. 10.

it."[7] Verbal behavior consists of stimulus-response associations which depend upon another organism for their reinforcement. These associations are usually the effect of multiple causes and show a great diversity of manifestations through recombinations. The reinforcement may come through a kind of subvocal conversation, the individual thus reinforcing his own behavior.[8] Any notion of "idea," Skinner says, is an "explanatory fiction," in that we build into the "idea" all the properties needed to explain the behavior.[9] "The speaker is merely the *locus* of verbal behavior, not a cause," and "knowing what one is saying" is on the same level as knowing anything else in the stimulating environment.[10] Similarly "meaning" is a misleading concept, as it is traditionally understood. "We must find," says Skinner, "the functional relations which govern the verbal behavior to be explained."[11] In conformity with the tenets of strict behaviorism, Skinner tries to limit himself to the physically observable.

With such complicated behavior, however, he soon finds himself in difficulties. According to Skinner's formulation, we cannot identify the stimuli which provoke verbal responses until we hear the responses themselves, because of the great complexity of the behavior and the fact that a speaker is also a listener reacting to his own behavior. As Skinner has said, "Part of what [the speaker] says is under the control of other parts of his verbal behavior. . . . The speaker qualifies, orders or elaborates his behavior at the moment it is produced."[12] Chomsky has commented on this theoretical inconsistency, pointing out that this drives the stimuli back into the organism, so that they can no longer be considered part of the outside, physical, observable world. Hence verbal behavior becomes quite unpredictable, and the relationship between stimulus

---

[7] B. F. Skinner, *Verbal Behavior* ("William James Lectures" [Cambridge, Mass.: Harvard University Press, 1948]), p. 10.

[8] Skinner (1957), p. 10.

[9] *Ibid.*, pp. 6–7.

[10] Skinner (1948), p. 95.

[11] Skinner (1957), p. 10.

[12] *Ibid.*, p. 10.

and response cannot be shown to be lawful. Skinner is therefore forced into a use of the terms *stimulus* and *response* which is inconsistent with his own definitions of them in his experimental work. Chomsky comments, "One would naturally expect that prediction of the behavior of a complex organism (or machine) would require, in addition to information about external stimulation, knowledge of the internal structure of the organism, the ways in which it processes input information and organizes its own behavior. These characteristics of the organism are in general a complicated product of inborn structure, the genetically determined course of maturation, and past experience."[13] Here Chomsky's ideas run parallel to those of Miller, Galanter, and Pribram in *Plans and the Structure of Behavior*. These writers maintain that speaking requires "a motor Plan [in the sense in which "plan" is used in connection with computers] to be constructed very quickly and efficiently, not by rote, but by the operation of a higher-level Plan that (has) this motor Plan as its object."[14]

The view that there is more to speaking than to other forms of behavior is also held by the group of Soviet psychologists who base their work on the theories of Pavlov and Vygotskij. Pavlov did not believe that classical conditioning as he had studied it in dogs applied to the speech functions of man. He maintained that there are two signal systems—conditioned stimuli (the objects of the surrounding world and their features) which act directly on man, and "words, word-groups and connections arising on the basis of them" which are peculiar to man. To Pavlov, "it was the word which has made men of us," because through the word man has achieved a new type of neural activity—abstraction. These psychologists disagree entirely with Skinner's view that verbal behavior does not differ in any significant way from other behavior, stating that, on the contrary, it has a directive effect on other behavior

---

13 Noam Chomsky, review of B. F. Skinner's *Verbal Behavior*, in *Language*, XXXV (January-March, 1959), 27.

14 G. Miller, E. Galanter, and R. Pribram, *Plans and the Structure of Behavior* (New York, 1960), chap. xi.

and transforms it. A. R. Luria and his collaborators have done extensive experimentation in this area and have concluded that "speech restructures the cognitive processes of man, enabling him to get a profound orientation in surrounding reality, to distinguish essential features and relations, and to systematize his accumulated experience." Because of this active, directive role of speech, conditioning in man is quite a different process from conditioning of animal behavior: "The reaction does not need to be reinforced every time, the stage of initial generalization may be absent, connections are easily altered, reactions may be established to abstract features, etc. . . ."[15]

A number of psychologists at different periods have regarded as too rigid and unrealistic the strict behaviorist position of considering only the physically observable stimulus and response. Hilgard recounts that Woodworth in his early days urged that the S-R (stimulus-response) motto be hung on the walls of the psychological laboratory as a constant reminder to the students, but that he "later modified his S-R motto to read S-O-R, recognizing that the mediating processes in the organism always had to be taken into account in the correlation between stimulus and response."[16] There is now considerable interest in the modified behaviorist position of such psychologists as C. Osgood and O. Hobart Mowrer, who give an important place to mediating processes in their theoretical formulations.

Osgood, in particular, has reinstated meaning in verbal behavior, explaining it as "a representational mediation process," which is a distinctive part of the total reaction to an object that has become conditioned to the word for that object or to the visual perception of the object. This mediating "meaning" acts as a self-stimulus causing the individual to react in a particular way to the real object,

---

[15] This account of the theories of Soviet psychologists has been drawn from the review of B. F. Skinner's *Verbal Behavior*, by O. K. Tikhomirov of the Department of Psychology of the University of Moscow, in *Word*, XV, No. 2 (August, 1959), 362–67.

[16] E. Hilgard, *Theories of Learning* (2d ed.; New York, 1956), p. 464. The S-O-R formula was proposed first by Dashiell in 1928.

this reaction frequently taking the form of linguistic responses.[17] "Meaning," then, is the product of the individual's learnings and experience. "Some of these learnings depend upon the reinforcement he has had from other individuals in his speech community—these are the learnings which have made him know what is commonly 'meant' or 'denoted' by the linguistic item . . .; other learnings depend upon experiences which may be more or less unique to him but which may have common elements with the experiences of others."[18]

Mowrer would take this theory of mediation one step further, maintaining that the "representational mediation process" at the heart of verbal behavior is that part of the total reaction to an object which has become conditioned to secondary motivation (i.e., fear or disappointment) or secondary reinforcement (i.e., hope or relief) which have been temporally contiguous with a previously neutral stimulus (e.g., a word). Therefore, for Mowrer, there is a strong element of emotion in "meaning."[19]

Mowrer is not alone in emphasizing the part played by emotion in verbal behavior. Much of the research of Osgood, Suci, and Tannenbaum on the semantic differential (an instrument for measuring meaning) deals with the affective dimensions of meaning,[20] and others have emphasized the important role emotion plays in a child's learning of his native language.[21] As G. Miller has pointed out, the child's early words are probably "used to designate objects only secondarily and their principal function is to express the emotional state of the child."[22] M. M. Lewis in his study of

---

[17] C. Osgood, "Studies on the Generality of Affective Meaning Systems," *American Psychologist*, XVII (January, 1962).

[18] J. B. Carroll, review of Osgood, Suci, and Tannenbaum, *The Measurement of Meaning* (Urbana: University of Illinois Press, 1957), in *Language*, XXXV (January-March, 1959), 74.

[19] O. Hobart Mowrer, *Learning Theory and the Symbolic Processes* (New York, 1960), p. 71.

[20] C. Osgood, G. Suci, and P. Tannenbaum, *The Measurement of Meaning* (Urbana, Ill., 1957).

[21] Dorothea Johannsen also emphasizes this aspect of language in her paper on the "Ontogenetic Development of Language," given at the Tufts University Seminar, 1961.

[22] George A. Miller, *Language and Communication* (New York, 1951), p. 148.

How Children Learn to Speak makes a similar observation. The child learns his early words, he says, in a "complicated and intricate pattern of experience, where "the expressive behavior of the speaker" (usually the mother he loves), and "the rich diversity and intricacy of the situation" play important roles. "Nothing could be less 'neutral' for the child. The word comes to him charged with emotion, as much a part of his experience of his mother at this moment as her physical presence. . . . So that when . . . the phonetic pattern of the word comes to stand out for him in this experience, it carries for him a richness of emotional experience, in addition to the expressiveness lent to it by her voice."[23] These observations support Mowrer's autism, or self-satisfaction, theory of the learning of the "mother" tongue by the child: Mowrer maintains that the child reproduces words in the absence of his parents "as a means of recapturing some of the pleasures which parents have previously provided,"[24] a contention which is supported by a number of clinical studies.[25]

There would appear then to be two distinct schools of thought among psychologists on the nature of language: the behavioristic school in the Watsonian tradition, represented by Skinner, which takes account only of the physical manifestations of language that are outwardly observable, and the neo-behavioristic which allows place for mediational and emotional processes that are not directly observable but may be inferred, and even studied, from their overt manifestations. It follows that methods of foreign-language teaching based on the first of these will differ from methods based on the second. It is the contention of the writer that the audio-lingual methods are based on the Skinnerian theory, and it is from this basic theoretical position that their advocacy of "mimicry-memorization" in pattern drills and dialogue learning has been derived.

---

[23] M. M. Lewis, *How Children Learn to Speak* (London, 1957), pp. 73 ff.

[24] Mowrer (1960*b*), p. 80.

[25] *Ibid.*, pp. 79 ff. (quotations from Mowrer's paper on "The Autism Theory of Speech Development and Some Clinical Applications" [1950]).

It is thus that they have been able to visualize, as Politzer and others have done,[26] a method in which meaning would be completely ignored,[27] and have consistently advocated that in the early stages of foreign-language learning the role of understanding should be minimized as much as possible,[28] the major emphasis being on the development of automatic responses. Attention is devoted primarily to the processes which theoretically should produce the most effective foreign-language habits and only secondarily to the individual, who is reacting in his own way to the teaching methods and who therefore provides the factor in the situation which will ultimately determine whether the language is learned or not.

---

[26] Politzer (1961), p. 19, quoted above (p. 20). In "The Language Laboratory as a Teaching Machine," F. Rand Morton says, "Meaning, and particularly lexical meaning, may be virtually excluded in the elicitation of response," in *Language Teaching Today*, ed. F. Oinas (*International Journal of American Linguistics*, XXVI, No. 4, Part II [October, 1960], 159).

[27] This parallels the abstract approach to language analysis of linguistic scientists such as Joos and Chomsky. Chomsky says, "Meaning is a notoriously difficult notion to pin down. If it can be shown that meaning and related notions do play a central role in linguistic analysis, then its results and conclusions become subject to all of the doubts and obscurities that plague the study of meaning, and a serious blow is struck at the foundations of linguistic theory" (Report on the Sixth Annual Round Table Meeting on Linguistics and Language Teaching, Georgetown University, 1955).

[28] See quotations appended to Assumption 1 in chap. iii.

V

ASSUMPTION 1

FOREIGN-LANGUAGE LEARNING IS BASICALLY A
MECHANICAL PROCESS OF HABIT FORMATION

BEHIND the first assumption that foreign-language learning
is a mechanical process of habit formation, and Corollaries
1 and 2, that habits are strengthened by reinforcement of
the right response as it occurs, lies a Skinnerian concept of
conditioning. Simches and Bruno have made this psychological basis explicit in their paper on "A Psycholinguistic
Rationale for FLES," stating that "language is acquired
through habit. This implies that it must be taught by producing appropriate stimuli and responses. In this response
kind of learning, we must also remember that in order to be
learned a response must be performed; moreover the response is learned more effectively when it is immediately
rewarded . . . . The type of behavioristic conditioning
described above is important to all FL [foreign language]
learning."[1] Skinner continually emphasizes these same elements and has used them as the basic operating principles
of his teaching machines. This "response kind of learning,"
says Brooks, "makes no pretense of being communication"[2]
(that is, it is limited to the outward manifestations of verbal
behavior, as is consistent with a strict behaviorist position),
and it is continued to the point of saturation or automatic
performance (that is, until the association between stimulus
word, or phrase, and response has become a habit as a result

---

[1] Tufts University (1961), p. 4.
[2] Brooks (1960), p. 142.

31

of frequently rewarded repetition). The reward, or reinforcement, in the language-learning situation comes from the approbation of the teacher, or, in the case of work in the language laboratory, from the satisfaction of hearing one's own version corroborated by the version of the model.

Skinner divides the processes of learning into two types: Type S (classical conditioning) and Type R (instrumental learning), but he considers that the first rarely appears in pure form and is not of great significance. In his experimentation, he has concentrated on Type R, instrumental learning or the conditioning of operant behavior (that is, "behavior that has an effect upon the environment which has a return effect upon the organism").[3] In this type of learning, no conditioning can take place until the response to be conditioned is emitted in the first place. It is the conditioning of this emitted response as operant behavior which is of interest to Skinner, not the nature of the stimulus which initiated it. Once the response has been emitted, it is instrumental in obtaining some form of reward. In a human learning situation this would be secondary reward such as praise or the satisfaction of achievement. This reward, or reinforcement, increases the probability that this instrumental response will recur, and repeated reinforcement establishes it as a habit, liable to extinction only if it occurs and is not rewarded on a number of occasions.

In a foreign-language learning situation, Skinner's paradigm would work in the following way. The student emits a foreign-language response which is comprehended and thus rewarded by the reinforcement of the teacher's approval. It is now likely to recur, and, with continued reinforcement, it becomes established in the student's repertoire as an instrumental response, capable of obtaining certain satisfactions for the student in the form of comprehension and approval in classroom situations. It is even more strongly reinforced if by means of it he obtains what he wants in a foreign-language environment. Plenty of opportunity to use it and receive more satisfactions and reinforcement preserve the response from extinction, at least while the student is

---

[3] Skinner (1957), p. 20.

still at school or in a position to use it instrumentally. The audio-lingual techniques seem to meet this situation adequately, as they provide plenty of opportunity for the student to use foreign-language responses in the classroom situation and to receive the reinforcement of acceptance and comprehension. So also do the techniques of certain other methods, such as the Direct Method.

Basic to all operant conditioning is the principle that the response must occur before it can be reinforced. Skinner says in *Verbal Behavior*, "Any operant, verbal or otherwise, acquires strength and continues to be maintained in strength when responses are frequently followed by the event called 'reinforcement.' "[4] Here as elsewhere, however, he does not attempt to explain how the response comes to be emitted in the first place. In his research, Skinner has consistently taken the position that operant behavior can be examined and understood without attention to the stimulus which originally caused the response to be emitted. As this first response cannot appear spontaneously from the student's repertoire in a foreign-language learning situation, there would seem to be a definite advantage in combining Type S (classical conditioning) and Type R (instrumental learning) in one sequence. Yet foreign-language acquisition cannot be fitted into a pure classical conditioning paradigm either, because in this type of learning the original response which is conditioned is a natural response to a natural (unconditioned) stimulus. This may apply to native-language learning, but it is inappropriate to foreign-language learning. Mowrer's revised two-factor theory seems to meet this situation more efficiently, but with a completely different interpretation of the effect of reinforcement and a distinctive use of the word "habit."

Mowrer refuses to accept a view of habit which regards it as a "fixed, automatic, unconscious neural connection or bond between some stimulus and some response," asserting that "most behavior . . . is under voluntary control" and that "learning does not fixate particular actions or movements in any mechanical, automatic fashion."[5] Mowrer

---

[4] *Ibid.*, p. 29.
[5] Taken from the phonograph record accompanying Mowrer (1960*a*).

maintains that "learning is related, exclusively, to the connections involved in the *informational feedback* from a response or response 'intention' (i.e., a partial or perhaps symbolic occurrence of the response) and that it involves no change in what may be called the 'executive' (brain-to-muscle) pathways in the nervous system."[6] This "informational feedback" comes from the stimuli (internal and external or environmental) associated with the response (i.e., response-correlated stimuli), and it is these stimuli which arouse the emotion of hope, which is secondary reinforcement, thus causing the individual to *want* to make the particular response. "It is only the relative *attractiveness* of the response . . . that is altered by learning: and *this* alteration is unequivocally assumed to be neurologically based."[7] This "attractiveness" reminds us of Lewin's "positive valence" (attraction of a perceived goal-object), and Tolman's "positive cathexis," which is a similar concept. Both of these also develop from learning. Mowrer himself says that " 'habit' is a set of 'valences' rather than a drive-response 'bond.' "[8]

The occurrence of a response does not depend, therefore, upon similarity between present and past objective situations, but on whether the response "produces response-related stimuli which have 'cathexis' relevant to the organism's current *needs*."[9]

In the classroom, the current need of the student may be to please the teacher, in which case repetition of the learned response produces response-correlated stimuli associated with previous teacher approval which therefore have cathexis or attraction. If the response is to have such cathexis in foreign-language communication outside of the classroom, the response-correlated stimuli must also be associated with the pleasure of making oneself understood in communication, thus arousing hope. This element is lacking in a drill session or in the language laboratory where the tape cannot react with comprehension but can only give an opportunity for verification of the correctness of the re-

[6] Mowrer (1960*a*), p. 220.
[7] *Ibid.*, p. 221.
[8] Mowrer (1960*b*), p. 30.
[9] Mowrer (1960*a*), p. 286.

sponse. Such verification may well be one of the student's current needs, and the laboratory practice period, like the drill, of considerable value, but both must be supplemented by communication experiences where desire to be understood is satisfied.

Habit strength is "a function of *how many* of the stimuli produced by a response possess *how much* of this so-called reinforcing potential. If this potential is extinguished *or* if the stimuli which a given response usually arouses are, by whatever means, prevented from occurring, it is assumed that the 'habit' will be obliterated forthwith, whatever the state of the S_d-R_i connection," (drive-produced stimulus–instrumental response connection).[10] Learning does not alter what the individual can do, but rather what he "*wants* and wants to *do* (and does)."[11] All too often the student who has been understood in the classroom where the situation required an obvious and well-learned response and for whom the response-correlated stimuli of foreign-language words and phrases has aroused hope, ceases to try to speak in the foreign language and reverts to the native language when he finds he is not understood in communication. Such has been the experience of many tourists who have studied stereotyped phrases of a foreign language to which teacher and fellow students responded readily, but who became discouraged when the accustomed comprehension was not forthcoming abroad. If our students are to persist in their efforts to use the language in communication, broader training than repetitious drill will be needed. The subject of such training is discussed fully in chapter viii.

According to Mowrer's formulation, foreign-language learning would occur as in the following description. The native-language word or phrase has already been conditioned to some part of the meaning of an object or event with which it is temporally contiguous in a rewarding situation, so that stimuli associated with this word or phrase arouse hope of further reward (this is secondary reinforcement), and the response tends to recur.[12] The foreign-language word or

10 *Ibid.*, p. 228.
11 *Ibid.*, p. 220.
12 For a full explanation of this process, see chap. xii.

phrase may be conditioned to the object or event by the same process of conditioning as the native-language word by being temporally contiguous with it in a rewarding situation, as advocated in the Direct Method, or, if contiguous even for a short time with the native-language word or phrase in a rewarding situation, it may be conditioned by second-order conditioning to the existing concept of the word or object to which the native-language word refers.[13]

In this way, stimuli associated with the reaction to the new word become conditioned to hope of further reward, and the word is used instrumentally to obtain this reward (which may be teacher approval, prestige with peers, or the satisfaction of being able to understand and be understood in the foreign language). In other words, the stimuli which are associated with the use of the foreign-language word become associated ("correlated") with the rewarding situation and therefore provide a *hopeful* "feedback," which encourages the continued use of the word. The more it is used in rewarding situations, the more these response-correlated stimuli which have acquired secondary reinforcement (or hope-arousing) powers are intensified, thus facilitating the tendency to make this particular response in similar situations (environmental stimuli adding further to the intensification). In this way a "habit" is developed. To Mowrer, "habit" is response facilitation, and it is the secondary reinforcement (the emotion of hope) which constitutes the "habit."[14] This explains why the response occurs not automatically but selectively when hope is aroused by the response-correlated and environmental stimuli.

---

[13] The writers of the A-L M materials, by giving an English rendering of the dialogues which are to be memorized, have recognized the oft-suspected fact that in a pure Direct Method class the child may subvocally pair the foreign-language word with the nearest equivalent in his own language, even if he does not do so vocally, and that it is probably better therefore to guide the student in this process rather than to ignore its existence. Thus, they try to show that the two languages do not run parallel, and that only part of the native-language meaning can be absorbed into the new meaning. The dangers which must be kept in mind in such "pairing" will be considered in the examination of the fourth assumption in chap. xii.

[14] In the foregoing description the word "relief" may replace "hope" as another form of secondary reinforcement. This would apply in the case of an anxious student.

Mowrer's theory also accounts for the extinction of wrong responses. A response which is punished by a painful experience, such as the disapproval of the teacher, embarrassment in the presence of fellow-students, or lack of comprehension, arouses stimuli which are conditioned to the emotions of fear or disappointment (secondary motivation), and these lead to response inhibition and passive avoidance behavior. Thus, when the student is about to give the previously punished response, the stimuli associated with its production (and, in a classroom situation, environmental stimuli as well) provide a warning "feedback" and the response is not given.

A situation familiar to language teachers is the great difficulty experienced by the nervous child or the child with poor auditory discrimination in speaking and understanding the foreign language. Such children may be able to read and even write the language well, but they cannot utter the words in front of other people. This is explained very well by Mowrer's theory. In the early stages of language study, these students have experienced fear, anxiety, or acute embarrassment and disappointment in trying to use the foreign language (or even, at an earlier stage, the native language) [15] in the presence of other students or the teacher, and these emotions have become conditioned to the stimuli associated with oral language responses, thus inhibiting their production. If such emotional inhibitions are to be avoided, there must be a relaxed and encouraging atmosphere in the language classroom in the early stages, and the teacher will need to develop skill in correcting language responses without embarrassing or humiliating the student. It would seem that the language laboratory should provide a solution to this problem, but work in an isolated booth does not associate the emotion of hope with face-to-face situations and so does not provide the complete answer.

---

[15] B. Harleston has suggested, in "Learning Theory, Language Development, and Language Learning," that research could profitably be conducted on the characteristics of the native-language learning of good and poor foreign-language learners. He hypothesizes "that many of the characteristics of language learning and performance are similar in the two cases" (Tufts University [1961], p. 36).

Practice is still needed in using the language successfully in the presence of others.

According to Mowrer, then, the word is acquired as the student hears or repeats it (i.e., becomes acquainted with it) in a rewarding situation in temporal contiguity with either the native language word or the object or event to which it refers. This explains "latent" acquisition of vocabulary and language patterns as well as active acquisition. These new verbal responses will still be associated with certain sensory, response-correlated stimuli. These stimuli may be either environmental (spoken by another, but heard by the student) or associated with the student's own response (i.e., sensory stimuli from the student's own production of sounds which are similar to those associated with the original speaker's utterance). Such stimuli will facilitate the recurrence of these foreign-language words as active responses at a later date, because they will be conditioned to hope aroused by the reward or reinforcement of earlier occasions. This parallels the way many new words and phrases are acquired throughout our lives in our native language.

Further application of these two fundamentally different concepts of habit, both based on the same body of experimental data, to the problems of foreign-language learning will show that the basic psychological orientation of the promulgators of a teaching method must influence vitally the type of method advocated, just as the psychological assumptions of two teachers ostensibly using the same method will lead to noticeable differences in classroom practice. It is for this reason that classroom teachers are the despair of any reformer trying to impose a uniform teaching method. Each teacher has his own psychological approach, explicit or implicit, which has emerged from his individual experiences in teaching situations.

Pattern drill, as described and advocated in the sources, certainly meets Skinner's requirements that a response must be emitted in order to be reinforced and must be instrumental in obtaining reinforcement a number of times in order to become habitual. Therefore, in accordance with this psychological orientation, students should repeat the correct response many times, having it reinforced by approval, until the habit is clearly established. Yet Mowrer says that "responses, in the sense of overt, behavioral acts are never 'learned' " and that "all learning is in the nature of stimulus substitution" (i.e., the substitution of response-correlated stimulation for the stimuli which originally produced the response).[16] It is "through conditioning or associative shifting, that stimuli take on their inner meanings for the individual, that signs and situations acquire their significances. Meanings . . . constitute for the individual a sort of inner subjective field; and it is this on-going, ever-changing motivational state which, moment by moment, modifies, controls and directs behavior."[17] Mowrer's revised two-factor theory, then, emphasizes the internal rather than the external "field" as "the dynamic, energy-producing, causally effective source of behavior."[18] This view has certain parallels with that of the Soviet psychologist Luria, that voluntary behavior in man is directed by speech-processes, sometimes external but at other times what he calls "inner speech." This concept of "inner speech" seems to be akin to Mowrer's "inner subjective field" of meanings. Luria also calls it "inner connections which lie behind the word" and which have a "selective effect in directing . . . motor responses."[19] Just as Mowrer maintains that "responses in the sense of overt behavioral acts are never 'learned' " and therefore are not dependent on quantity of reinforcement, so Luria insists that in man a reaction does not need to be reinforced every time it occurs because of this directive power of man's higher psychological function of speech.[20]

If Mowrer's theory is accepted, then unremitting and intensive drill is seen for several reasons to be much less desirable as a way of learning a foreign language. Instead of increasing learning, in the hands of all but the most adept teachers it can cause boredom by sheer quantity of reinforced acts; tedium may become a punishing effect and so develop

[16] Mowrer (1960a), p. 386.
[17] Ibid., p. 310.
[18] Ibid., p. 311.
[19] A. R. Luria, "The Directive Function of Speech," Word, XV, Part II (August, 1959), 351.
[20] Tikhomirov (1959), p. 367.

a negative feedback from the response-correlated stimuli. The continual demanding of automatic responses to stimuli relies entirely on external stimuli related to the exchange and completely ignores that inner "field" of meanings and the "on-going, ever-changing motivational state" of which Mowrer and some of the Gestalt psychologists speak. These should be drawn into service in the establishment of language habits by repetition in meaningful situations rather than in an artificial drill situation "making no pretense of being communication."[21] The response, in the ideal learning situation, becomes associated with many stimuli, internal and external, and its selective reproduction will thereby be facilitated. If the student is made to depend solely on external stimuli, the probability of the recurrence of the response in a spontaneous foreign-language situation will be low if these stimuli are not reproduced specifically as they were drilled. Similarly, work in a language laboratory, as the central element of a foreign-language course, does not provide the response-correlated stimuli of a face-to-face situation, with the rewarding aura of such features as tone of voice and facial expression, as they are associated with gestures and other elements of what has been called "paralanguage" and "kinesics."[22]

If Mowrer's theory of habit is accepted, then both pattern drill and language laboratory practice should be auxiliary and subordinate to practice in natural, face-to-face situations, contrived in the classroom, in a relaxed atmosphere where the student feels free to express himself on subjects associated with his everyday life and that of his fellow-students. As Mowrer says, "The total 'field,' psychologically speaking, . . . consists of both extrinsic and response-correlated stimuli and their attendant meanings; and these meanings are being constantly collated, compared, and organized into 'choices,' i.e., specific actions and inactions."[23] A method which does not allow for these "choices" is not making full use of the student's potential.

---

[21] Brooks (1960), p. 142.

[22] These same response-correlated stimuli account for the way students remember the words of songs in the foreign language, and this is another valuable aid to language learning.

[23] Mowrer (1960a), p. 342.

The dialogue method, as advocated by the audio-lingual sources[24] is intended to develop a more flexible knowledge of the language, more directly useful in everyday situations than that developed in pattern drills. The technique advocated consists of learning the dialogue by heart, at first in small sections consisting sometimes of as little as two or three lines for one lesson, drilling these to the point of automatic reproduction before learning more lines, and continuing in this way to the point of automatic repetition of the complete dialogue. This procedure makes the dialogue method only another, albeit a more elaborate, type of mimicry-memorization drill. After thorough memorization of the dialogue, the A-L M units allow for "dialogue adaptation," where students use the same material in new combinations of questions and answers. When conducted with imagination, this can provide the realistic give-and-take of a conversational situation, so long as students are permitted to adapt the dialogue sentences to their own interests in quizzing classmates or teacher. "Directed dialogue," where the teacher suggests exactly what the students should say in both question and answer, reverts again to a purely external situation remote from any expression of the student's own "meaning." An example taken from Level One of the A-L M materials for French will serve to illustrate this point:

Teacher: Pierre, demandez à André où il va passer les grandes vacances.

Pierre: Où est-ce que tu vas passer les grandes vacances?

Teacher: André, répondez-lui que vous allez au bord de la mer.

André: Je vais au bord de la mer.[25]

A better opportunity for the type of face-to-face experience which an application of Mowrer's theory would indicate appears to be provided by the "Conversation Stimulus" at the end of each A-L M unit. Based on material already

---

[24] The technique for the use of this method is set out in full detail in the *Teacher's Manual* (1961), pp. 11–13, 23.

[25] *Teacher's Manual* (1961), *French, Level One*, Unit 14, p. 8.

learned, it allows room for some imagination. Conducted by a teacher with a manner which puts the students at their ease, this could supply some of the kind of practice envisaged. In a relaxed atmosphere, with the student allowed some selective choice of material and language, the reinforcement of hope (or expectancy) is conditioned to the internal and external stimuli associated with his utterance (i.e., hope of being understood and of being able to communicate acceptably) and so facilitates their recurrence.

Some of the more recent audio-lingual materials[26] provide a large number of recombinations of the basic dialogue which re-create lively situations suitable for classroom dramatization. If these are learned and acted by various groups of students, they can, through dramatic identification, develop the response-correlated stimuli of a meaningful, face-to-face situation of which we have been speaking. If, however, they are merely used for further group memorization and repetition or as reading practice, either of which ignores the nature of communication, their value will be considerably reduced.

Mowrer says that learning alters what the student wants to do, rather than what he can do,[27] thus making incentive motivation an important element in the learning process. Even intensive pattern drills and dialogue learning will not make the student produce foreign-language phrases appropriately unless he wants to produce them. In a face-to-face situation, interestingly contrived, it is natural for him to want to communicate, and learning takes place in these circumstances. The foreign-language teacher is faced with a double problem, first, of providing the student with the correct formulae of expression in the new language, and second, of arousing a desire to communicate in that language. As both are essential for a genuine, personal interchange of ideas, the most efficient classroom method must be one which provides the necessary stimulation for development in both of these areas.

---

[26] *Ecouter et Parler, Entender y Hablar, Verstehen und Sprechen* (New York: Holt, Rinehart, & Winston, Inc., 1962).

[27] Mowrer (1960a), p. 220.

VI

TWO LEVELS OF LANGUAGE

THE DISCUSSION of differing theories of habit formation has clearly shown the nature of the cleavage that exists between certain schools of psychological thought on the operation of verbal behavior. Is "'knowing what one is saying' on the same level as 'knowing' anything in the stimulating environment," as Skinner puts it?[1] Is the speaker "merely the *locus* of verbal behavior, not a cause,"[2] the control going back to the environment and to the history of the organism? If this is so, then "the acquisition of oral and aural ability, in a second as in a first language, is primarily a mechanical rather than an intellectual process."[3] If, however, language is more than external stimulus and response and intraverbal association; if, as Lashley maintains, a selective or scanning process is operative that is related to the integrative functions of the cerebral cortex,[4] then some exercise must be provided in the language class for this aspect of verbal behavior.

Skinner himself refers to two levels or systems of verbal behavior, one based upon the other, the upper system seem-

---

[1] Skinner (1948), p. 96. See also Skinner (1957), p. 313.

[2] Skinner (1948), p. 95; Skinner (1957), p. 313.

[3] F. Agard and H. Dunkel, *An Investigation of Second-Language Teaching* (Chicago, 1948), p. 281; this is stated to be "the cardinal principle" of the experimental oral-aural (audio-lingual) methods being investigated.

[4] K. Lashley, "The Problem of Serial Order," in *Cerebral Mechanisms in Behavior—the Hixon Symposium*, ed. L. Jeffress (New York, 1951), p. 130. Also available in S. Saporta (ed.), *Psycholinguistics: A Book of Readings* (New York, 1961), pp. 180–98.

ing to guide or alter the lower; but he refuses to admit of any difference in operation of the two systems. "The upper level," he says, "can only be understood in terms of its relations to the lower," and even "the highly complex manipulations of verbal thinking can . . . be analyzed in terms of behavior which is evoked by or acts upon other behavior of the speaker."[5]

This theme of two levels of verbal behavior figures prominently in some of the recent literature on language. Osgood speaks of "meaning" as a mediating response (r_m) which causes self-stimulation leading to overt response behavior which may be linguistic (R_v, organized in instrumental skill sequences).[6] Chomsky cites a number of instances of verbal behavior in children and adults, such as the construction and comprehension of utterances which are quite new, and the detection of slight distortions in print, which "indicate that there must be fundamental processes at work quite independently of 'feedback' from the environment."[7] Lashley discusses "a series of hierarchies of organization" in language, finding indications that "elements of the sentence are readied or partially activated before the order is imposed upon them in expression, (suggesting) that some scanning mechanism must be at play in regulating their temporal sequence."[8] He admits, however, that he has no idea of the nature of this selective mechanism.

This notion of a selective mechanism has been developed in much greater detail by Miller, Galanter, and Pribram in *Plans and the Structure of Behavior.* "Behavior," they say, "is organized simultaneously at several levels of complexity."[9] Using the cybernetic model (an analogical comparison between minds and computers), they work out the thesis that man has, through language, "the capacity to use Plans to construct Plans to guide behavior"[10]—again a hierar-

---

[5] Skinner (1957), p. 313.

[6] C. Osgood, *Method and Theory in Experimental Psychology* (New York, 1953), p. 699.

[7] Chomsky (1959), p. 42.

[8] Lashley (1951), pp. 121, 130.

[9] Miller, Galanter, and Pribram (1960), p. 15.

[10] *Ibid.*, p. 157. The word "Plan" is used in this book in the sense of computer program.

chical organization. ("Plan" is defined as "any hierarchical
process in the organism that can control the order in which
a sequence of operations is to be performed.")[11] In this way,
one Plan, representing the strategy, sets in motion subordinate Plans, or tactics, as these are appropriate to the over-
all strategy.

Since the days of Watson, psychologists have been wary
of any explanations of behavior which seemed to be teleological, but purposefulness has become less suspect since
scientists have shown that "machines with negative feedback (are) teleological mechanisms . . . that . . . (can)
strive toward goals, (can) collect information about the
difference between their intentions and their performance
and then work to reduce the difference."[12] This extraordinary capacity of machines is based on a hierarchy of plans
which set other plans in operation—a selective, scanning
mechanism—and much of the work on machines has been
based on careful study of human thought processes.[13] By
man, as by machine, "external messages are not taken *neat*,
but through the internal transforming powers of the apparatus. . . . The information is then turned into a new form
available for the further stages of performance."[14] The
strict behaviorist school has always maintained that, no
matter how complex, thinking is finally a matter of muscular action—subaudible speech or covert muscular response. Keller and Schoenfeld, who base their work on verbal
behavior firmly on that of Skinner, state that "we all
think, but we do so with our muscles which provide the
only S[D]'s (drive-stimuli) for the tact 'thinking.' "[15] Skinner
himself prefers not to "make guesses about the muscular or
neural substratum of verbal events," but speaks of "physiological mediators,"[16] presumably between stimulus and re-

---

11 *Ibid.*, p. 16.
12 *Ibid.*, p. 42.
13 *Ibid.*, pp. 42, 163, 168, 172. Footnotes on these pages give very
useful references to work in this area.
14 Norbert Wiener, *The Human Use of Human Beings* (Boston,
1954), pp. 26–27.
15 F. Keller and W. Schoenfeld, *Principles of Psychology* (New
York, 1950), p. 390. The Skinnerian term "tact" is defined on p. 386.
16 Skinner (1957), p. 435.

sponse. As a result of this type of theory, psychologists have come to look upon language behavior as consisting of associative chains of reflexes and have theorized on the probability of one word's generating any other particular word in the chain. Lashley quotes M. F. Washburn as seeing in language "a combination of movements so linked together that the stimulus furnished by the actual performance of certain movements is required to bring about other movements."[17]

Some psychologists and students of language have rebelled against this approach and have argued that were language merely reference this position might be maintained, but syntax indicates a complicated form of organization at work. Lashley sees "behind the overtly expressed sequences, a multiplicity of integrative processes which can only be inferred from the final results of their activity."[18] Words are influenced by other words quite remote from them in the sentence, and often we must keep the whole sentence in our heads before comprehending the first part of it. On the other hand, what is to come will frequently change the form of what precedes it. People, even young children, are able to generate completely new utterances which they have never heard before. Miller, Galanter, and Pribram observe, "We cannot yet say how a talker selects the content of his utterances. But even within the relatively narrow scope of syntactics it is clear that people are able to construct and carry out very complicated Plans at a relatively rapid pace."[19] Particularly striking is the way in which children, without explicit instruction, "acquire essentially comparable grammars of great complexity with remarkable rapidity."[20]

In view of all these facts, it seems difficult to maintain a belief in one level of language behavior of a mechanical character. Yet if the idea of two levels is accepted, provision must be made in the teaching of a foreign language for training at both levels. "A mechanical process of habit

[17] Lashley (1951), p. 114.
[18] *Ibid.*, p. 115.
[19] Miller, Galanter, and Pribram (1960), p. 154.
[20] Chomsky (1959), p. 57.

formation" can apply only to the lower level of manipulative skill, important as this is. It is interesting to examine the work of several psychologists who have developed, and experimentally tested, theories involving two types of learning, to see the degree to which they correspond with these two levels of thought and mechanical skill. Although these experiments were not specifically related to foreign-language learning, they provide interesting material for extrapolation.

Let us look first at the work of Katona, a Gestalt psychologist. Katona carried out a number of experiments on learning by two methods: "direct practice" of specific subject matter without understanding the relationship between items and steps, and the "method of understanding," in which certain structural principles were developed from the successive steps of learning. With the latter method, Katona says, "The subjects developed an integrated knowledge to which all parts of the practice period contributed."[21] The results of these experiments showed that material was better retained for longer periods when it was learned with understanding and that new problems were solved with much greater facility. By this method, the specific solutions of set tasks were not learned as such, but as examples. Katona says, "We do not learn the examples; we learn *by* examples. The material of learning is not necessarily the object of learning: it may serve as a clue to a general principle or an integrated knowledge."[22]

If we extrapolate from this to foreign-language learning, we can see the validity of the method of direct practice for learning certain mechanical associations (subject-verb combinations, noun-adjective agreements, tense endings, time sequences, and common patterns such as negative and interrogative forms). Here it is appropriate, as Katona suggests, to "isolate the material of learning, interfere with the possibility of its spreading, and exclude the understanding of inherent relations,"[23] until its use has become automatic.

---

[21] G. Katona, *Organizing and Memorizing* (New York, 1940), pp. 109, 111.
[22] *Ibid.*, p. 125.
[23] *Ibid.*, p. 126.

This parallels the rationale behind the pattern drill procedure. To develop ability to handle syntax as a whole in a meaningful way, however, requires a different technique, one which will develop "a plasticity or flexibility of learning which permits reasonable applications on a wide scale."[24]

Direct practice leads to transfer where identical elements are involved, as Thorndike found as early as 1903. Learning with understanding, however, leads to transposition, a Gestalt concept, where "the elements are changed, but the whole-qualities, the essence, the principle are preserved in recollection . . . and we may apply them under changed circumstances."[25] More attention must be given to this type of learning in the foreign-language class if the students are to develop fluency in all kinds of language situations. This subject is discussed in greater detail in chapter xi, in connection with the third major assumption.

Another interesting theory of two types of learning is elaborated by Neal Miller and John Dollard in *Social Learning and Imitation*. The basic theoretical orientation in this case is Hullian, and therefore, behavioristic, the essential element in learning being drive-reduction. Learning is considered to follow certain definite psychological principles, sheer practice not being of itself sufficient. For a connection to be strengthened, certain conditions must prevail. "The learner must be driven to make the response and rewarded for having responded in the presence of the cue. In order to learn one must want something, notice something, do something and get something."[26]

Building on this theoretical basis, Miller and Dollard describe two forms of learning by imitation: matched-dependent behavior and copying behavior. The source of each of these is acquired motivation. As a result of the experiences of social life, the individual tends to feel anxiety at being different and relief at being the same as others. This acquired drive moves him to copy activities of which society approves or which others seem to be enjoying.[27]

---

[24] *Ibid.*, p. 136.
[25] *Ibid.*
[26] Miller and Dollard, *Social Learning and Imitation* (New Haven, Conn., 1941), p. 2.
[27] *Ibid.*, pp. 162–63.

The essence of matched-dependent behavior is that responses are connected to a cue from the leader. Because of his superior learning, the leader is able to discriminate this cue, but the follower cannot, and so the follower is rewarded for following the cue of the leader. This seems to parallel the drill approach in the language class, where the student, the neophyte, is led to imitate the teacher as closely as possible without being given any explanations which would help him to discriminate the cues to which the teacher, who knows the foreign language, is responding. The student's behavior is reinforced by approval and self-satisfaction when he follows the teacher's lead. This seems particularly appropriate to the very early stages of foreign-language learning, but is too restrictive if continued to an advanced stage, because it can lead only to identical-elements transfer (that is, the ability to produce the appropriate response to a stimulus which reappears in exactly the same form in a new setting, a situation which is by no means certain to occur in a natural foreign-language exchange). In this way, matched-dependent behavior is consonant with the "direct practice" described by Katona.

The second type of imitation is copying behavior, where the follower learns to model his behavior on that of another, through responding to cues of sameness (for which he is rewarded by reduction of anxiety), and to cues of difference (which increase the strength of the anxiety drive). During this learning period, he is made aware of the band of tolerance within which his action is acceptable as a match for the model act by the reactions of an external critic who rewards and punishes sameness and difference. As a result, the copier becomes aware of the discriminative cues and so is able to act as his own critic, thus advancing his learning by his own efforts, without further need of a teacher or critic.

This approach in a foreign-language situation would closely approximate Katona's "learning with understanding." The discrimination training in sameness and difference would make the student aware of the "whole-qualities" to be sought. It seems particularly appropriate to the question of the teaching of pronunciation, but it is also relevant to the teaching of syntactic formations, enabling the student to acquire the "feel" of the language and of the thought-molds in which it is cast. Miller and Dollard emphasize the fact that the essential difference between copying behavior and matched-dependent behavior is that in the former the copier is responding to cues produced by stimulation from his own behavior, which he has learned to discriminate, as well as to those from the model's responses, whereas in the latter the copier is dependent on the leader's superior knowledge. Copying behavior thus makes it possible for the individual to act as his own critic in different situations. He takes, as it were, his teacher along with him and so can continue to learn independently. It would seem essential for the foreign-language teacher to make the student aware of what he is doing and train him in the discrimination of his own errors. This is particularly important if the language laboratory is to play a major role in the foreign-language course, and if practice at home is to be a valuable exercise.

Although it is artificial to suggest that these models of learning form exact parallels, it is interesting to note that psychologists from two such divergent schools of thought make a similar major distinction between levels of learning: a mechanical level, and a level which involves understanding of how one is learning and of the essential elements of what is being learned. As the theme of this book develops, it will be seen that these two levels must both find a place in the design of the foreign-language course if students are to learn to use the language accurately and flexibly in all kinds of situations.

VII

COROLLARY 1
HABITS ARE STRENGTHENED BY REINFORCEMENT

BASIC to the Skinnerian theory of habit formation is the concept of reinforcement or reward. According to Skinner, reinforcement is essential if habits are to be strengthened and the probability of their recurrence increased.

This concept has been basic to behavioristic psychological theories since Thorndike's Law of Effect, which stated that "when a modifiable connection is made and is accompanied by or followed by a satisfying state of affairs, the strength of the connection is increased."[1] Punishment has not been found to have a strictly opposite effect, but it may be considered rather to induce the individual to do something else which makes him less likely to repeat the punished action.

In studying reinforcement, Skinner does not take up the question of the nature of the stimulus which produces a response; rather, he concentrates on the observable phenomenon that once a response has been emitted the probability of its recurrence is increased or decreased by its effect. If it is not reinforced by a satisfying or rewarding state of affairs, then it will tend not to recur and so will gradually disappear from the individual's repertoire by the process of extinction. In a learning situation, this rewarding state of affairs has been equated with knowledge of results (success or failure),[2] and Skinner has worked this informative aspect

---

[1] Hilgard (1956), pp. 19–20.
[2] Experimental evidence of the value of knowledge of results with

51

of reinforcement into his teaching-machine methods, so that the student is encouraged at the completion of each step by the knowledge of his success. This is also the theoretical assumption behind the language laboratory method of enabling the student to hear his own version of a foreign-language utterance through his earphones and then the correct version of the native speaker from the tape. It is emphasized by Brooks in his summary of approved classroom procedures, when he advocates "the shortening of the time span between a performance and the pronouncement of its rightness or wrongness, without interrupting the response," because "there appears to be, by immediate feedback, a reinforcement of the right response if it is immediately known to be right."[3]

A single occurrence of a response, if rewarded, may, according to Skinner, be sufficient to establish a habit, although this will probably be a weak one until further occurrences have been reinforced. This principle has been the basis of Skinner's very successful work in animal training by successive approximations. As the animal tends to repeat what it was doing at the time of reward or reinforcement, the trainer is able, by "baiting" each step, to lead the animal to perform a whole series of actions just as he desires.

Secondary reinforcement, not primary, is the important element in the development of verbal behavior after very early childhood. The concept of secondary reinforcement is based on conditioning. A stimulus that was not originally reinforcing or rewarding in itself can become reinforcing through repeated association with a stimulus that is reinforcing. Through conditioning it has acquired the power to condition.[4] As this concept has been developed by Skinner, secondary reinforcers may be money, social acceptance, or advancement in one's position, or (in a foreign-language situation) the approving words of the teacher or the admiration of other students.

---

human subjects is given in R. Woodworth and H. Schlosberg, *Experimental Psychology* (rev. ed.; New York, 1954), pp. 686 ff.

[3] Brooks (1960), pp. 138, 206.

[4] Keller and Schoenfeld (1950), p. 232.

Such reinforcement, then, provides the clue to the application of Skinner's method of successive approximations to the learning of a foreign language. As an example, we may take audio-lingual discrimination learning, in classroom or language laboratory, by which students are trained to make finer and finer distinctions between sounds which at first seem to them to be identical. By approving, and thus rewarding, successive approximations to the correct foreign-language sound, the teacher should be able, after a period of time, to lead the student closer and closer to an acceptable version of this sound. As the response must occur in order to be reinforced, it is essential that the students make the foreign sounds themselves as often as possible, rather than merely hearing them or hearing about them. The necessity for careful monitoring in the language laboratory now becomes obvious, if Skinner's principles are accepted; otherwise unmonitored students will be reinforcing the sounds they make with the satisfaction of accomplishment long before they have reached any acceptable approximation of the native-language sound. The valuable training of successive approximations does not occur by chance.

Applying Mowrer's principles to the same situation, we may say that the response-correlated stimuli from the repeatedly rewarded sounds will arouse the emotion of hope and so increase the probability of their recurrence. From this standpoint also it becomes imperative to insure that the sounds made are as correct as possible as often as possible, and that only sounds acceptable to a native speaker are being reinforced in this way.

Other behaviorist psychologists also emphasize the value of reinforcement, but, unlike Skinner, they take up the question of what causes the response to be emitted. Hull and Neal Miller, for instance, emphasize the importance of primary and acquired drives in producing responses. For Hull, a specific need of an organism produces a primary drive, the level of which depends on the level of all other needs of the organism at the particular time. If a stimulus-response connection leads to reduction of this drive, this connection is reinforced as a consequence. Later, under the influence of Miller's research, Hull tended to accept Miller's version that it was reduction of the stimulation associated with the drive that was reinforcing (i.e., "food in the mouth" as against "food in the stomach"). It is this drive-stimulus reduction theory that is of most interest in foreign-language teaching, particularly as it applies to acquired drives.

According to Miller, any strong stimulation can act as a drive or motivating force, and he speaks of secondary or acquired drives as a theoretical complement to secondary reinforcement. Neutral stimuli associated with primary drive-stimuli acquire the properties of secondary drive-stimuli. Hence anxiety may be considered an acquired drive, and it is a potent motivating force in many social situations, among them the learning situation. This secondary drive of anxiety may be reduced by the secondary reinforcement of reassurance or approval. This seems to fit in very well with the applications of Skinner's system which have already been discussed. Although, like the research of Skinner, that of Hull and Miller was not directed to foreign-language learning, we can draw some interesting observations from it by extrapolation of principles which apply to learning in general. Turning attention to the properties of the stimulus, it throws further light on the question of reinforcement in foreign-language learning.

First, if rewards reduce acquired drive stimulation (such as anxiety), then they can also, after a certain point has been reached, reduce the drive-stimulus to zero. As a result the individual will turn to other behavior. It is important to keep this in mind in foreign-language teaching, where a great deal of discrimination training is necessary. If language responses which would be unacceptable to a native speaker are rewarded too readily, the student's anxiety about the perfection of his work will be reduced and the unsatisfactory responses will remain strongly intrenched in his repertoire. Being dominant, they will make different responses less likely to occur. This is a danger with un-monitored laboratory work. As Miller and Dollard have pointed out, it is often necessary to force the student into a "learning dilemma," where these inadequate responses will not be sufficiently rewarded to reduce his anxiety and he will therefore be forced to try new ones.[5] This throws the responsibility on the teacher, however, to watch the situation carefully, in the light of his understanding of his students, in order to see that this withholding of reward is not carried to the point where the student feels discouraged. Such discouragement may so increase his anxiety that it becomes a very strong drive, the intensity of which can cause resistance to extinction of the inadequate responses and so interfere with new learning.[6]

As a result of research on animals, K. W. Spence, a more recent exponent of Hull's system, has moved from the idea of a reinforcer strengthening associations between stimulus and response (increasing "habit strength") to the idea that the presence of a reinforcer increases incentive motivation (or the desire of the individual to repeat the act).[7] Spence's concept of incentive explains how a reinforcer can be satisfying, depending on whether a motivating condition is present which makes it attractive to the individual, or whether the experience of the individual is such that this reinforcing situation is recognized as potentially satisfying. If we extrapolate from this to human behavior, it would appear that, in a foreign-language situation, a mechanical application of some standard reinforcement which does not take into account the student's perception of the goal of foreign-language skill cannot of itself be automatically reinforcing. If the student has not been led to feel any need which can be satisfied by foreign-language skill or has not glimpsed the possible satisfactions of knowledge of another language, then some real ground-work must be put in before the routine reinforcement of "success" or "failure" can be of any significance.

On the other hand, the attractiveness of the incentive object may be so great that the individual feels frustration in being unable to attain it, and this will lead to increased

[5] Miller and Dollard (1941), pp. 33–34.

[6] J. McGeoch and A. Irion, *The Psychology of Human Learning* (New York, 1952), p. 208.

[7] K. W. Spence, *Behavior Theory and Conditioning* (New Haven, Conn., 1956), pp. 133–37.

stimulation and a heightened activity level. In this way, the incentive object may have a drive-enhancing effect, as Spence has shown, rather than a drive-reducing effect.[8] Foreign-language teachers who know how to make their subject active and exciting have observed this effect on students not at all linguistically gifted, who will work very hard in order to remain in the foreign-language class. In such cases as this, the incentive effect is not negative, in the sense of satisfying needs or reducing a drive, but positive, in exciting the individual to active response.[9]

It would seem clear from all these studies that the action of reinforcement is by no means automatic in habit formation, but must vary a great deal in effect from individual to individual. As early as the work of Thorndike, emphasis had been placed on the active role of the learner, who comes to the learning situation with needs and problems which determine what will be satisfying to him.[10] This aspect of reward has been studied carefully by the Gestalt and field theorists. Koffka, for instance, devoted a great deal of thought to the individual's "behavioral environment," pointing out that the individual's perception of things about him, and their attractiveness and unattractiveness for him, reflect his own attitudes, needs, and abilities. Koffka's behavioral environment is organized (in accordance with Gestalt principles), and therefore for him individual behavior is governed not directly by external stimuli but by the way they impinge upon and are accepted or rejected by this internal organization.[11] The behavioral environment is an important element of what Lewin calls "the life space," within which there may be locomotion toward a situation which satisfies a need. What this situation is depends upon the individual's perception of his environment and how it can meet his needs, that is, upon "the interrelationships among past achievements, momentary goals, social atmos-

---

[8] *Ibid.*, p. 135.

[9] A very useful discussion of the subject of incentives is to be found in McGeoch and Irion (1952), chap. vi.

[10] Hilgard (1956), p. 23.

[11] R. Woodworth, *Contemporary Schools of Psychology* (rev. ed.; New York, 1948), pp. 137–42, provides a very readable account of Koffka's ideas.

phere, and individuality."[12] It is the individual's view of his environment that directs his selection of goals and his redefinition of them as he goes along.

This Gestalt view depends too much on inferences about what goes on under the surface of human behavior for the behaviorist psychologists, who prefer to restrict themselves to the physically observable, but it is interesting to see that its implications are not so very different from those of Spence and Mowrer. It reflects facts of behavior which cannot be ignored. What is reinforcing or rewarding to one individual may not be reinforcing to another individual in the same situation, because it may not be perceived by him as a reward. As Lewin has pointed out, perception of something as a reward (or as success or failure) depends on the degree to which the individual sees it as related to his personal goals and also to his level of aspiration, his momentary goals. These goals may well be a reflection of his cultural background, as well as his individual interests and needs, and it may be necessary for the teacher to convince him of the value of spending time in learning a foreign language. In this, the teacher is often battling family attitudes which have strongly influenced the student.

Tolman brought out a related aspect of the reward situation in his concept of "goal expectancy." He found experimentally that animals seem to have an expectancy of specific goal objects, and, if these are not forthcoming, objects which would normally be rewarding to them cease to have that effect and become frustrating instead.[13] Experiences of everyday life make it reasonable to extrapolate from these results to human behavior. With respect to foreign-language learning, students expect or are led, by either teachers or persons outside the school, to expect certain achievements. If teaching is oriented so that these goals are not reached, then what is achieved will not appear rewarding and so will cause discouragement or frustration. If, for instance, students expect or are led to expect that drill methods and memorization will develop their powers of communication in the foreign language, and if these meth-

---

[12] Hilgard (1956), p. 278.
[13] *Ibid.*, p. 192, gives a description of these experiments.

ods do not lead to facility in normal conversational situations, they will experience such discouragement and frustration.

For any foreign-language teaching method to be effective it must take these facts into account. It cannot be assumed that the long-range goal of eventual conversational facility in a foreign language, or the immediate goal of being correct in an utterance, will of themselves be sufficient incentive, or be perceived as sufficiently rewarding, to carry a high-school student over months of tedious drill and meticulous sound-discrimination exercises. Politzer admits that this can be a problem with audio-lingual methods, adding that "the teacher as well as the student must be convinced of the necessity of pattern drills."[14] The Agard-Dunkel investigation also noted this problem, observing that "as drill-sessions succeed each other with relentless regularity, as the material becomes more and more difficult to assimilate, many begin to tire or to lose interest and fail to apply themselves to the extent the method demands in order to assure continuing success . . . ; boredom sets in."[15] This is surely a picture of the reaction of students who do not perceive the reward as the teacher perceives it, and who find even the momentary goals irrelevant to their needs and interests. Yet foreign-language lessons can be varied in content, full of interest, even colorful and exciting, with use of a variety of techniques. All of these techniques may not, theoretically, be as efficient as drills and memorization, but the gain in maintaining the students' enthusiasm and personal enjoyment will lead to greater attainments as students work with a will at the more tedious aspects of the subject. The students will be rewarded at short intervals by the satisfaction of achieving momentary goals, goals which are relevant to their own needs and interests, and thus will be kept working toward the more distant goal of language mastery.

Rewards may be extrinsic or intrinsic to the student's own perceived goals. If the reward is extrinsic, it may fail to establish an effective habit. If the reward is really intrinsic, however, we can speak of success or failure, rather

---

14 Politzer (1960), p. 19.
15 Agard and Dunkel (1948), p. 292.

than reward: the individual achieves his goal and this is in itself satisfying. Thorndike had already accepted this Gestalt emphasis, referring to it as the "belongingness" of rewards.[16] When the reward really "belongs," in this sense, the student will "want" to repeat the rewarded act and a habit will be established which will be strengthened in the future, if it continues to help the student to achieve his goals, or weakened, if these goals subsequently change. (In this case, the reward is no longer satisfying, and the habit gradually becomes extinguished through lack of reinforcement.)

Lewin has pointed out also that success has to be measured in terms of what the individual is trying to do. Depending on each individual's level of aspiration, a feeling of success may be experienced on reaching the goal, on coming close to the goal, on making progress toward a goal, or even on mere selection of a socially approved goal.[17] Experienced teachers will immediately recognize students belonging to each of these four groups. Unfortunately, with the new emphasis on foreign-language learning, a certain number of foreign-language students come into the last category, feeling "successful" because they are actually being taught a foreign language, irrespective of whether they are learning a great deal.

What is success for one is not an experience of success for another. Understanding these individual differences in level of aspiration is part of the technique of the master teacher, and careful distinctions can be made in a classroom situation which are not possible when standardized materials are presented to all students without distinction in language laboratories or teaching machines. It follows that work in the language laboratory should be carefully supervised by the classroom teacher and integrated into the work of the classroom, so that it appears to be truly relevant to the aspirations of the students. Where feasible, adjustments may be made to standardized materials used in the laboratory to allow for two, or even three, levels of difficulty, so that the drill work will appear neither too easy and

---

[16] Hilgard (1956), pp. 28–29.
[17] *Ibid.*, p. 276.

repetitious to the more gifted members of the class nor too difficult for the weaker students, but each group may have an experience of success which will increase desire to repeat the rewarded acts.

By sympathetic handling of students in the classroom and laboratory, based on an awareness of their present perceived goals, the teacher alone can best encourage them to see intrinsic value in higher goals and can challenge those whose goals are already high to define even more closely the region of difficulty within which they experience success.

The perception of goals can also determine success or failure in the use of the dialogue method. With this in mind, the teacher will make sure that students understand where the method aims at taking them; otherwise, a student with a low level of aspiration in foreign-language behavior may feel a completely satisfying sense of achievement in being able to "rattle off" a dialogue, without being able to use the language material contained in it in any meaningful way, the activity becoming a goal in itself. The teacher must induce the student to so perceive the goal of fluent foreign-language behavior that a tension system is set up, and the student will not relax his efforts until he achieves this goal or his own close approximation to it. Such a goal becomes a positively valenced objective and will carry the student over the hard and tedious work involved in reaching it—making even work attractive because of the intrinsic nature of the goal reward.[18]

Any discussion of the factors involved in reinforcement and reward brings out the necessity, as Bernard Harleston has recently observed, for further study of the practical question, "What conditions of reinforcement can be effectively manipulated to produce and maintain second language learning?"[19] It is apparent from the foregoing discussion that such conditions will vary from class to class. The foreign-language teacher must understand his students and their needs if he is to insure genuine reinforcement of their efforts.

---

[18] A full discussion of Lewin's studies of goals and rewards will be found in Hilgard (1956), pp. 274–80.
[19] Tufts University (1961), p. 44.

VIII

COROLLARY 2
FOREIGN-LANGUAGE HABITS ARE FORMED MOST EFFECTIVELY BY GIVING THE RIGHT RESPONSE, NOT BY MAKING MISTAKES

THE SECTION on reinforcement has brought out the fact that when the required response occurs and is reinforced a number of times, the probability of its recurrence increases steadily. This has been shown to be the case whether one accepts the explanation of the Law of Effect or of the conditioning of the emotion of hope. From the teacher's point of view, the more frequently the correct response occurs the more economical is the teaching procedure. As Politzer says, "The real skill of the teacher lies not in correcting and punishing wrong responses but in creating situations in which the student is induced to respond correctly."[1] This has been the basis of many effective teaching procedures in foreign-language classes: choral recitation of responses by the class after the teacher before individuals are called on to recite; drills and exercises in which a minimal change has to be made; question-and-answer procedures in which the student's response involves, for the most part, repetition of materials contained in the question; and the use of memorized dialogue material in re-creations of everyday situations. Such procedures insure that the student repeats aloud a great deal of foreign-language material with a very low probability of error.

---

[1] Politzer (1960), p. 14.

The main procedures advocated by proponents of the audio-lingual method are of this type: pattern drill, dialogue memorization, directed dialogue, and recombination narrative.[2] Whether in the classroom or in the language laboratory, these procedures approximate what Miller and Dollard have called matched-dependent behavior, where the student is carefully copying the actions of the teacher-model in every particular, trusting to the teacher's superior knowledge and understanding of the requirements of the situation.[3] At this stage, generalization enters in. In behaviorist psychology, the term "generalization" refers to the process which occurs when one stimulus, which is to some degree equivalent to another, can substitute for it in arousing a conditioned response. By this process of generalization to other similar situations in which the response is made without the guidance of the teacher and is still rewarded, this response becomes independent. In its simplest form, generalization occurs the first time the student who has learned to greet his teacher and classmates in the foreign language returns home and greets his parents with the newly acquired foreign-language formula. He is rewarded by their pleased surprise and then proceeds to use it with other people.

Matched-dependent behavior does not parallel in all ways Skinner's model of operant or instrumental conditioning. In operant conditioning, several random responses occur before the subject hits upon the one which the experimenter has decided will be the "right" one. Even after the rewarding of the "right" response, wrong reactions occur frequently before the habit becomes established and the subject has learned the discrimination which brings the reward. The habit does become established after a time and, with increase in the occurrence of rewarded repetitions of the "right" response, it is strengthened and established.

In an operant conditioning situation, the animal has no

---

[2] Directed dialogue is illustrated in chap. v. Recombination narrative combines vocabulary and structures of preceding units in a new form with some variations and some new words which are easy to recognize as cognates or by context.

[3] Miller and Dollard (1941), pp. 92–97.

effective choice. The experimenter has decided what is the "right" response and the animal must find it. This is one way in which Skinner's operant conditioning does provide a parallel with foreign-language learning, because neither the student nor the animal is in a position to decide which is the right response. The student's responses must conform to the arbitrary system of the foreign language in order to be "right." It is manifestly better, therefore, that the beginning student be provided with a model of the correct response which he can imitate as in a matched-dependent situation, rather than be left to try and work out his own version. In trying to find the correct response, his choices will be based on his previous experience with his native language. When the English-speaking student, without much experience of the foreign language, is allowed such freedom of choice, the inevitable result is an undesirable crop of Anglicisms. In the matched-dependent situation the student establishes, through steady practice, a hierarchy of responses, certain responses becoming dominant at the appearance of certain cues. This makes for speed in responding to these cues, which, in both pattern drill and dialogue memorization, have been written into the materials as being the most frequent and most useful in the language.

In all languages, a study of usage reveals certain associations common to all speakers of that language, that is, certain "stable patterns of response built up by reciprocal reinforcement in much the same way for all speakers of one language."[4] The presence of these conversational tags, common associations, and recurrent sequences of words becomes obvious in word-association experiments and is the basis of some lie-detector tests. When a student is learning a foreign language these common associations are lacking, and he is greatly hampered in his efforts to construct authentic utterances.[5] Pattern drill and dialogue

---

[4] G. Miller (1951), p. 185.

[5] A valuable device which could be more fully exploited in this regard is the use of word-association games in the classroom. Carefully prepared, these would supply a relaxing end-of-class activity, while building up associations which are essential to the development of fluent speech in the foreign language.

memorization help to establish these associations and so give the student a basic repertoire.

The common complaint about this matched-dependent type of learning is that it does not develop ability to speak fluently in an unstructured situation where the learned stimulus does not appear exactly as it did in the structured situation and where new and unpracticed responses are appropriate. It is most suitable for the early stages of foreign-language learning, when the framework of common associations must be established. Fernand Marty, who has experimented with several variations of the audio-lingual approach, has come to the conclusion that dialogues are valuable mainly for purposes of motivation. "This ability to communicate effectively within some stereotyped conversational areas increases the student's confidence," he says, "and contributes to keeping his motivation high throughout the foundation course. . . . These dialogues do not, however, prepare students who can use the language as an effective tool to express their *own* ideas."[6]

It will be interesting to see whether theorists other than the reinforcement theorists have anything to say about the practicing of right responses. Corollary 2 will be found to be consistent with the principles of all the major theorists, but each emphasizes a different aspect of the situation, thus suggesting certain modifications in classroom methods which may bring us nearer to the desired outcome of foreign-language fluency.

E. R. Guthrie, for instance, maintained that temporal contiguity was the most important factor in learning and that the occurrence of the response constituted the learning of it, reinforcement merely acting as a factor which prevented the subject from trying other responses and thus "unlearning" the desired response.[7] The more frequently the desired response occurs, the less likely are other responses to be learned in its place. With a complicated skill like learning a foreign language, according to Guthrie, each

---

[6] F. Marty, *Linguistics Applied to the Beginning French Course* (Roanoke, Va., 1963), p. vi.

[7] See Hilgard (1956), chap. iii.

small part of a correct sequence must become associated with its cue, and so a correct sequence will gradually be developed through practice. The making of mistakes is the learning of undesirable responses which will have to be eliminated, and this elimination can be achieved by causing the desired response to occur in the presence of cues which originally called forth the undesired response. Guthrie's theory of one-trial learning requires the arrangement of the learning situation so that the stimuli or cues provided will call out the right response. So long as these cues recur, the right response will also recur. Mistakes must be eliminated by careful study of the cues leading to these responses and practice of the right responses in the presence of these cues. Guthrie's theory supports the method of practicing classroom drills with minimal changes, devising remedial drills where necessary, but it also demands foreign-language cues in class which will later be reproduced in an out-of-class situation. Pattern drills, class exercises, and dialogues should therefore be couched in the language which the student will meet in an everyday situation, because exercises in an artificial language which will never be used outside of the classroom are useless in preparing the student for fluent use of the language. The audio-lingual materials have taken this into account and have tried, on the whole, to avoid that artificiality for the sake of practicing grammatical structures which is to be found in some other textbooks.

By its emphasis on cues as the key element in the recurrence of the right response, Guthrie's theory makes it clear that classroom practice must reproduce as nearly as possible the atmosphere and behavior of real-life conversational situations, with subject matter which is relevant to the interests and activities of the individuals taking part, and be conducted in a congenial atmosphere approximating as closely as possible that of friendly discourse. The creation of such an atmosphere and the development of appropriate materials is a challenge to the imagination and sensitivity of the teacher.

E. Tolman would also accept the assumption behind

Corollary 2, while refusing to accept the idea of reinforcement as strengthening or establishing a habit.[8] To him, rewarding the right response represents confirmation of the hypothesis or expectation of the individual. It is not the main factor in the development of a habit, although with repeated experience it may determine when and where a learned act will be performed by increasing the attractiveness of the goal. Thus the student learns to discriminate which foreign-language phrases will achieve his purposes in which circumstances. In this way, Tolman's theory supports the notion that it is necessary to give the student practice in using foreign-language phrases successfully in a variety of situations, but it also warns the foreign-language teacher against placing too much reliance on practice as a method of building up habits. According to Tolman, continued practice after a response has been learned tends to fixate this particular response, making it harder for the individual to vary it on future occasions. In view of the fact that in most languages there is a variety of possible ways of expressing any one thing, too much "overlearning," as advocated by the audio-lingual sources, may fixate stereotyped responses and make it harder for the student, at a more advanced level, to develop flexibility in handling synonymous phrases and parallel constructions.

Gestalt theory has its word to say about the right response. According to classical Gestalt theorists, the most important effect on learning of repetition of the right response is the opportunity it provides for the individual to see relationships and so to restructure the field according to the "belongingness" or "requiredness" of these relationships.[9] It is advantageous for the student who is practicing by repetition to understand what he is doing, so that his understanding, as well as the mechanical association of words and phrases, may be strengthened. This does not support the attitude of the audio-lingual sources toward drill, as has already been shown in the discussion of the methods of direct practice and of understanding in chapter vi.

[8] *Ibid.*, chap. vi.
[9] *Ibid.*, p. 252.

In summary, we can draw from the major psychological theories the following guidelines for the maximum effectiveness of drills which involve repetition of the right response:

Drills should involve responses to cues which approximate those which may occur in a real-life situation.

The right response should be practiced in a situation where the reward shows it to be an effective way of achieving a goal, that is, where it is effective as communication in a variety of situations.

Whereas repetition is useful in establishing a response, "overlearning" can fixate stereotyped responses and reduce the student's ability to select among possible alternatives.

Practice of the right response should be conducted in such a manner that the student understands in what way the response is "right," which will facilitate the transfer of the response to appropriately similar situations.

Since the audio-lingual method stresses repetitive practice of patterns and common word sequences, it will be interesting to examine in more detail the results in other areas of learning of extensive research on drill and repetitive practice by Gestalt, behaviorist, and functionalist psychologists.

In *Productive Thinking*, Wertheimer quoted a number of investigations into the inability of children who were good at tasks in school to tackle other tasks involving the application of what had already been learned, and noted that there was an "emphasis on mechanical drill, on 'instantaneous response,' on developing blind, piecemeal habits," and concluded that "repetition is useful, but continuous use of mechanical repetition also has harmful effects. It is dangerous because it easily induces habits of sheer mechanized action, blindness, tendencies to perform slavishly, instead of thinking, instead of facing a problem freely."[10] He tells a story about a boy who said to his father, "You see, daddy: I am very good in arithmetic at school. I can do addition, subtraction, multiplication, division, anything you like, very quickly and without mistakes.

---

[10] M. Wertheimer, *Productive Thinking* (New York, 1945), p. 112.

The trouble is, often I don't know *which* of them to use . . . ."[11] This could be paralleled by the student who performs very well in a pattern drill session, and can repeat his memorized phrases perfectly in directed dialogue, but is at a loss to find correct ways of expressing his thoughts in a spontaneous conversation.

These views expressed by Wertheimer may be considered as representative of the Gestalt school.[12] The "blinding effect" he describes is explained in Gestalt theory as the result of the conditioning of the memory trace which makes it more and more available, with continued practice, for the reproduction of what has been practiced but, as a consequence, less and less available for use in other ways.[13] Gestalt theorists agree with Tolman that overlong repetitive practice can make the student inflexible.

Hull took the position that "repetition merely provides continued opportunities for the effective forces, whatever they may be, to operate."[14] Chief among these "effective forces" is reinforcement, which determines the course of such processes as generalization, discrimination, and extinction.[15] Experimentation showed, however, that there was a limit to the amount of repetition which was effective, even with reinforcement. According to Hull, after the habit has been established reinforced repetition does not increase habit strength but rather may have a decremental effect, because of fatigue.

Fatigue, or "that tired feeling," has been shown to be closely related to the morale of the individual and is not necessarily physical. The effects of fatigue are similar to the effects of what Hull has called reactive inhibition. According to Hull, reactive inhibition of learning takes place when contiguous repetition, demanding effort, continues for some time, with or without reinforcement.[16] In the case of reinforced but effortful learning, inhibition may

---

[11] *Ibid.*, p. 114.
[12] Cf. Katona (1940).
[13] Hilgard (1956), p. 233.
[14] Quoted in Osgood (1953), p. 328.
[15] For an explanation of these terms, see the Appendix.
[16] Mowrer (1960a), p. 401.

be attributed to the desire to reduce the primary drive of pain, or to physical fatigue. On the other hand, what the teacher thinks is reinforcement may not have a reinforcing effect on the student, as was shown in the discussion on reinforcement in chapter vii. With pattern drill, unless there is a set to learn the material and a positive attitude toward the drill on the part of the student, no reinforcement will be perceived and the effects of the drill will be interpreted as punishing. On the other hand, even with a set to learn, if the student experiences tedium and boredom through too much repetitive drill the approval of the teacher may cease to have a reinforcing effect, and knowledge of results may no longer be satisfying. Furthermore, if the student has a low level of aspiration he may reinforce his own responses with inner approval long before the teacher considers the drill completed; his drive level will be reduced; and he will feel "tired."

Elements in the development of fatigue are brought out in laboratory experiments on mental work described by Woodworth and Schlosberg.[17] Of these, we may take the following as providing material for reflection in relation to pattern drill and dialogue memorization:

a) Homogeneity of task may cause fatigue. If students are kept too long at rote memorization of foreign-language material, at drills (even of various types), and at repetition of dialogue material until perfection of recitation has been reached by all, then the task will become monotonous and actual learning will decrease. When dialogues are divided into small sections for memorization, as advocated for the Audio-Lingual Materials,[18] understanding of the total situation represented is greatly reduced and interest in it is difficult to maintain. Memorization of the few lines set for the day then becomes another memory chore like that of yesterday and the day before, and fatigue is likely to ensue. The teacher should vary activities during the class lesson and develop sensitivity to class reaction, so that the type of activity may be changed before tedium has set in.

It has been said that the teacher will be bored with drill

---

17 Woodworth and Schlosberg (1954), pp. 803–9.
18 *Teacher's Manual* (1961), pp. 12–13.

material long before the class tires of it,[19] and this has been given as a strong reason for use of the tireless tape in the language laboratory. However, this should not be taken to mean that students never tire. The danger of the tireless tape is that the students may be bored long before the tape wears out, and, unless the teacher is very attentive to the responses of the class in the laboratory, he may not detect the signs of fatigue quickly enough to avoid boredom. Laboratory practice is also a potential source of reactive inhibition, associating unpleasant experiences with oral language responses. Such fatigue in the laboratory may be obviated if periods of practice, especially at high-school level, are short and frequent, rather than long and infrequent. The material used for laboratory practice should be relevant to work being studied concurrently in the classroom, without merely repeating it. The possibility of fatigue resulting from homogeneity of task can be considerably reduced by thought and care in the preparation of the master tape, which should be designed to excite the student's interest by a new approach to old material and make demands upon him requiring some thought and active participation. An unexpected interlude will relax while adding variety and will set the student off with renewed energy on tasks that are basically similar to those that preceded it. It takes an imaginative teacher to keep the material of drills varied while still practicing the same structures, but imaginative teachers have always been the best foreign-language teachers, no matter what their method.

b) Fatigue often has an emotional rather than a physical basis. A student who is interested and experiencing success in his efforts will continue such efforts for much longer periods than his teacher would expect of him, whereas the student who is discouraged by failure, or who does not see value for him in what he is doing, will feel tired much more quickly than the teacher expects. As Bartley and Chute have said, fatigue may be "an attempt to escape or

---

[19] Northeast Conference (1961), p. 46.

retreat from a situation,"[20] a form of conflict resulting from frustration.

c) Fatigue can also result if a student is forced to maintain a rate of learning set by the teacher which is either too fast or too slow for him. In any class there is a great diversity of aptitudes and rates of learning, and in the foreign-language class particularly the differences become greater as the work becomes more advanced. Dunkel and Pillet give clear evidence of this in their description of their experiences with FLES at the University of Chicago Laboratory School. They point out that "foreign language study is homogeneous and hence cumulative. . . . The difficulties and confusions tend to become compounded."[21] It is difficult for the teacher to adapt the rate of presentation of material to all these different rates of learning, and so he is forced to strike an average rate, which may cause fatigue through boredom for the more intelligent and fatigue through frustration for those unable to learn at the rate demanded. Ideally, the language laboratory should solve this problem by enabling each student to proceed at his own rate, but many laboratory periods are unfortunately conducted as class lessons, rather than as opportunities for individual practice, and this ideal situation is not realized. Close supervision of laboratory work is essential, and it is easier if the class members are working on the same material at the same time. The teacher who is conscious of the serious problem of learning discrepancy should be able to plan the laboratory work so that a certain percentage of time is available for the student to work at his own pace on material that he personally needs most. Most laboratories are planned with complete facilities for individual work in the separate booths, or at least by rows, but often the teacher ignores this provision and chooses the easier way of supervising the laboratory lesson, thus sacrificing the maximum benefit to individual students. Yet it is obvious

---

[20] Woodworth and Schlosberg (1954), p. 805.
[21] H. Dunkel and R. Pillet, *French in the Elementary School: Five Years' Experience* (Chicago, 1962), p. 58.

that one of the advantages of the development of modern electronic aids is that they enable the student to work individually at his own pace and free the teacher from preoccupation with the whole class so that he may concentrate on helping individuals.

Fatigue has certain detrimental effects in the learning situation. It may cause the student to seek reward or satisfaction in relaxation which reduces the unpleasant effects of the fatigue, and he will then reduce the effort he is putting into learning. Or he may continue to put forward effort despite the fatigue, in which case he will tend to fix his attention on particular elements of the work to be learned, rather than on relationships within the work as a whole. In the latter case, his learning will be less available for transfer to other situations. From the point of view of performance, fatigue may cause him, quite unconsciously, to extend the "zone of indifference" within which a response appears acceptable, and so he will learn faulty language habits.

If pattern drill and dialogue memorization are to be efficient and effective methods of learning, it is as well for the teacher to be aware of these causes and effects of fatigue.

As Hilgard has pointed out, "learning always must remain an inference from performance and only confusion results if performance and learning are identified."[22] The perfection with which a class can repeat correct phrases after the teacher or language laboratory model, or even make minimal changes in drills, does not indicate degree of learning. Learning can be measured only after the student has demonstrated his ability to use these "right" responses in a variety of contexts, on a number of different occasions. A student who has always had the right response put into his mouth by the structuring of the learning situation can give an impression of glib fluency which may prove quite spurious when he finds himself on his own.

That students are unable to express themselves in unstructured situations has been a major complaint about

---

[22] Hilgard (1956), p. 3.

the audio-lingual methods, with their emphasis on repetitive learning and "overlearning" or "automatization of responses." In 1948, Agard and Dunkel observed that "while many students[23] could participate in memorized conversations speedily and effortlessly, hardly any could produce at length fluent variations from the basic material, and none could talk on unrehearsed topics without constant and painful hesitation."[24] In 1953, Carroll suggested, as a problem in need of further experimental research, "What psychological factors hinder students from passing beyond the mere repetition of set patterns to the more active stage of making variations in these patterns spontaneously?"[25] His question is still being raised by classroom teachers. Pattern drills and dialogue memorization which train students in producing the right response have not led automatically to fluency in varied situations, and this seems to warrant further examination of the principle of the right response.

Although, as has been shown, it is normally best to insure that the student does not make mistakes, this appears to be especially true at the lower level of foreign-language learning, where the student is learning to manipulate structures and make automatic agreements between various parts of speech according to the arbitrary patterns of the language. As has already been stated in chapter vi, language use consists of more than these manipulations. It is at the higher level of expressing his own "meaning" through the arrangement of structures that the student trained in automaticity of response is failing. Those who share Skinner's view that "ideas" are explanatory fictions and prejudicial to a discussion of verbal behavior[26] will immediately reject this suggested level as an unscientific concept, as misleading and extraneous to the discussion as the concept of "meaning,"[27] and will maintain that

---

[23] In the oral-aural experimental classes observed during the investigation from 1944 to 1946.

[24] Agard and Dunkel (1948), p. 288.

[25] Carroll (1953), p. 189.

[26] Skinner (1957), pp. 6–7.

[27] Ibid., pp. 9–10.

manipulation of language cues and responses is sufficient. They must then seek other solutions to the frequently observed problem of hesitancy and lack of fluency on the part of the student trained by memorization and repetition when he finds himself in an unstructured situation.

For mediation theorists, however, the student expressing his own meaning has no problems.[28] His meaning is related to his total experience, most of which has been associated with the signs of his native language. It is not surprising that he encounters difficulties when he tries to express part of his total experience with the limited number of foreign-language signs that he has acquired. If his experience with the signs of the foreign language has always been in structured situations where the foreign-language responses which are dominant in his repertoire have been the ones required, or where he could always follow the lead of a model, it is inevitable that, in an unstructured situation where he is thrown back entirely on his own resources, he will feel insecure and hesitant. In auditory perception, our expectations, based on verbal associations and knowledge of language structure, help us just as much as environmental cues. The student trained in structured situations has been accustomed to hearing material that nearly always realized his expectations and that, by the nature of the drill or of the dialogue variations, helped him to know what to expect. Now he is much more dependent on his ability to class the cues which he hears and to select from his repertoire the responses which are appropriate. As Osgood has pointed out, a stimulus is a compound affair. It is rarely the same in every detail from one situation to another, as it forms part of a larger pattern.[29] Osgood's observation is particularly applicable to a verbal situation. The student trained on well-drilled material is accustomed to distinguishing the cue in its familiar context and to finding the appropriate response from an equally well-drilled repertoire. Now he must select a response that will convey his meaning, not one that will fit the situation in an automatic sequence.

---

[28] See chap. iv.
[29] Osgood (1953), p. 724.

It is at this point that the breadth of training he has received becomes apparent. Has he been trained to recognize the crucial element in cues to which he has responded, or has his response been produced automatically and mechanically? This important issue will be discussed in detail in the examination of the third assumption in chapter xi.

Miller and Dollard have pointed out that in imitation learning there is a danger of becoming so attentive to the model, and so intent on correctness of imitation, that one's attention is not directed to the crucial factor which will enable one to perform the act independently in response to the environmental cues to which the model is responding. The student, they say, must learn to respond in the same way to a large number of different cue patterns, all containing the crucial element of which he has been made aware. This type of discrimination training they call "abstraction."[30]

Mowrer also emphasizes the importance of the stimulus becoming abstracted from or independent of the situation in which it first occurs. Abstraction can be achieved by discrimination training in a variety of different situations.[31] In pattern drill as advocated in the sources, explanations are not given until after command of the structure has been achieved, so that there is a distinct possibility of the student's imitating the model and producing the correct response without being aware of the crucial element. The "generalization," or grammatical explanation of the crucial element, which comes later, after practice, may not be absorbed by the student as fully as it might have been had he been made aware of it during practice. In the latter case, his period of practice would have provided an opportunity for abstraction as the crucial element reappeared in a variety of contexts. This does not mean that the crucial element must be presented deductively, with the teacher stating a grammatical rule and then giving the students practice in manipulating various examples of the rule. The structure may be presented first in several

---

[30] Miller and Dollard (1941), p. 72.
[31] Mowrer (1960a), p. 39.

contexts in the foreign language, and then a short discussion of the crucial element may ensue before more thorough practice is given. Finally, a generalization may be constructed by the class from their observations of the function of the crucial element during the drill or, in difficult cases, the teacher may give a generalization. This method provides opportunity for the student to develop a "meaning" for the crucial element, which would then, by mediated generalization, become available in wider contexts.[32]

A very important type of learning which corollary 2 seems to reject is what is commonly called trial-and-error learning, or, in Thorndike's term, "selecting and connecting." Without accepting Thorndike's connectionism, we may find his terminology helpful in this case.

As has already been noted, trial-and-error behavior is the basis of operant conditioning or instrumental learning, and many incorrect responses occur before the response which brings the reinforcement. Osgood has pointed out that it is a mistake to regard trial-and-error behavior as random behavior; it is rather "a narrow selection" from the individual's potential activity. "The more the response required is compatible with the physical situation, is transferable from previous learning, and is already associated with the existing motivation, the more probable is its occurrence and hence the greater the speed of selection by this method."[33] In other words, trial-and-error behavior is a definite effort to find a solution by using all the available resources as they are appropriate to the environmental situation.

So far in our discussion we have implicitly rejected trial-and-error behavior as a method of foreign-language learning on the valid premise that the foreigner has no way of knowing the arbitrary system of the new language without a demonstration by someone who does know it. This does not, however, rule out the possibility that there may be a place for trial-and-error learning when the

[32] *Ibid.*, p. 57.
[33] Osgood (1953), p. 308.

student has already acquired a certain basic knowledge of structure and vocabulary. As Miller, Galanter, and Pribram have pointed out, it is "not storage but retrieval, that is the real bottleneck in verbal learning."[34] Carroll, expressing the same idea in less metaphoric language, speaks of the "simultaneous and sequential 'choices' or 'decisions' made by the speaker" from the learned responses in his repertoire.[35] It is practice in retrieval, in making choices, that the student of the foreign language needs if he is to become fluent in an unstructured situation, and practice will involve making mistakes: trying out responses which will not always prove to be appropriate or accurate. Nor will trial-and-error or selecting behavior of this type always be performed with speed. Sometimes it will be fumbling behavior, as a response is tried tentatively and then rejected in favor of another, or as the student searches for suitable responses containing the crucial elements. These responses may not always be readily available because they may not be dominant in the hierarchy of responses he has built up through practice.

As Dunkel has pointed out, trial-and-error learning is a noticeable feature of the way we learn our native language,[36] and the child continues to make mistakes for months and sometimes years. In the learning of other skills too, we begin by making mistakes, which we gradually eliminate as we perfect our methods. The important thing is not complete avoidance of mistakes, but rather careful reinforcement of the correct response when it occurs and non-rewarding of the mistake, so that the probability of its recurrence will gradually diminish. Only through some form of trial-and-error experimentation in the classroom will the student have the opportunity to practice novel arrangements of the foreign-language forms he has learned, in circumstances where he can be carefully trained in correct discriminations. If he is continually in a situation where his responses are right and rewarded, he will never find himself in a learning dilemma where he must rearrange

---

34 Miller, Galanter, and Pribram (1960), p. 137.
35 Carroll (1953), p. 89.
36 Dunkel (1948), pp. 24–25.

his repertoire in order to meet new demands,[37] and he will not develop that adventurous spirit which will enable him to try to meet any situation by putting what he knows to maximum use. Such readiness to innovate, on the other hand, will lead to much more frequent expression of the student's thoughts in the foreign language and consequently much more reinforced practice in that part of language behavior which will be of most use to him in the foreign-language environment. This is what Carroll had in mind when he posed the question whether aural-oral methods might not be more successful "if, instead of presenting the student with a fixed, predetermined lesson to be learned, the teacher created a 'problem-solving' situation in which the student must find . . . appropriate verbal responses for solving the problem," thus being early forced "to learn, by a kind of trial-and-error process, to *communicate* rather than merely to utter the speech patterns in the lesson plans."[38]

Hockett, in his comments on adult language behavior, observes that in the native language "speech is broken up by pauses, by hesitations, by interruptions, by repetitions, by sudden changes of direction." Individuals "vary in fluency of control, and . . . the same speaker varies in fluency from one occasion to another. . . . Differences in fluency seem not to be differences of language habits in the proper sense, but rather of habits of some other order which are manifested, along with language habits, in speech."[39] Since this describes the use of a native language after many years of "overlearning," it would seem unreasonable to expect students in a conversational situation in a foreign language not to show the same hesitancies, incomplete or incorrect sentence structure, and changes of direction. If we keep these facts about native-language behavior in mind, we will be more tolerant of trial-and-error behavior in the foreign language.

By giving the student an opportunity to experiment with the new language in a variety of situations, we will be

---

[37] Miller and Dollard (1941), p. 34.
[38] Carroll (1953), p. 188.
[39] Hockett (1958), pp. 142–43.

helping him to achieve mastery at both levels of language behavior: at the manipulatory level, where he will be trained by repetition of the right response, and at the level of communication, where he will learn by experience in selection to apply what he has learned to new situations.

IX

COROLLARY 3
"LANGUAGE IS 'BEHAVIOR' AND . . . BEHAVIOR CAN BE LEARNED ONLY BY INDUCING THE STUDENT TO 'BEHAVE'"

PART I: MOTIVATION

COROLLARY 3 is a quotation from Politzer,[1] and it raises another important psychological question. The statement is based on the well-attested fact that we learn to speak a foreign language by speaking it, which is in accordance with reinforcement theory in which habit strength is built up by the number of rewarded repetitions of an act.

The interesting word in this statement, however, is "induce." As students are not puppets responding to the strings we pull, this brings up the basic question of motivation. What impels a person to behave in a particular fashion? As teachers, we cannot ignore this question, and a teaching method which appears on a sound theoretical basis may founder if it presumes that the student wants to do what his teacher wants him to do, especially at the high-school level, or that the mere doing of it implies that he is learning. As Thurstone pointed out as early as 1923, "Stimuli are responded to or disregarded according as they are relevant or irrelevant to O's [the organism's] ongoing activity."[2] At college level, many students pursue foreign-

---

[1] Politzer (1961), p. 2.
[2] Quoted in R. Woodworth, *Dynamics of Behavior* (New York, 1958), p. 36.

language studies as a requirement or as a basic tool for later purposes (study, professional reading, or travel) and are willing to trust the teacher's judgment as to the best way to achieve these goals efficiently. At high-school level, however, many students do not perceive so clearly the goals of language study, and it becomes imperative for the teacher to understand the role of motivation in determining the student's reaction to methods and materials. The teacher needs to see how he can best utilize the student's personal motivation, once he has identified it, and how he can redirect it if necessary. Psychologists agree that *most human motives are learned*, and this should be a source of encouragement to the teacher, who can aim at developing in the student the desire to learn the foreign language for its intrinsic interest.

Recent studies have stressed the importance of motivation in foreign-language study. In his study of "Foreign Language Learning Ability," Pimsleur has found "the two biggest factors . . . are the very general ones of verbal IQ and motivation,"[3] and Lambert's studies in 1961 point to the same elements: "Two independent factors underlie the development of skill in learning a second language: an intellectual capacity and an appropriate attitudinal orientation toward the other language group coupled with a determined motivation to learn the language."[4] These findings are not unexpected in view of a definition of motivation like that of McGeoch and Irion: "A motive or motivating condition is any condition of the individual which initiates and sustains his behavior, orients him toward the practice of a given task, and which defines the adequacy of his activities and the completion of the task."[5] This all-embracing notion of motivation is not held by these two psychologists alone. McDougall, Freud, Lewin, Woodworth, and Hull, to cite but a few, have each maintained

---

[3] Pimsleur, Stockwell, and Comrey, "Foreign Language Learning Ability," p. 16, in *Under-Achievement in Foreign Language Learning* (NDEA Contract OE-2-14-004, Report No. 1 [1961]).

[4] W. Lambert, *A Study of the Roles of Attitudes and Motivation in Second Language Learning* (Montreal, 1961), (NDEA Contract, SAE-8517 [Montreal, 1961]), pp. 155–56.

[5] McGeoch and Irion (1952), p. 194.

that all activity, except purely reflective action, is motivated.[6] There is a similar consensus that, as most motives in human subjects are learned, the previous history and the personality of the individual are important and must be taken into account in endeavoring to understand his motivation. Such highly personal motives as fear or anxiety, learned through past experience, may combine with learned social motives, such as desire for status in a group and for social approval, creating complex reactions which can work powerfully toward progress in a foreign language or toward inhibiting oral language responses.

Melton describes three functions of motivation. He states that motivating conditions energize the organism making it active, direct the variable and persistent activity of the organism, and emphasize or select the activities that are repeated (fixated) and those that are not repeated (eliminated).[7] This individual motivation is basic to all learning activities.

Different problems of motivation arise at the three stages of foreign-language study (launching out, getting to grips with the language, and consolidating lasting language habits at an advanced level), and these are worth examining in detail.

Many high school students do not begin foreign-language study on their own initiative and therefore may not perceive its relevance to their personal lives.[8] Their studies may be launched by college entrance requirements, availability of courses, social and family pressures, or mere curiosity. However, any of these reasons for study may be effectively incorporated into the student's personal motivation at the beginning of his foreign-language learning career, the family pressures acting as secondary drives to activity which is further stimulated by the incentive object of college entrance. As he proceeds, the sheer novelty of the subject matter and of the distinctive methods

---

[6] Woodworth (1958), pp. 48–55.

[7] Hilgard (1956), p. 340.

[8] The writer has vivid memories of teaching French in a public school in a dairy-farming district, where the study of a foreign language was a requirement for all students. Some of the boys protested vigorously, "But the cows don't speak French, Miss."

of foreign-language presentation awakens his curiosity or exploratory drive,[9] and all the colorful material available for introducing a new culture keep him alert and active, at a stage when the level of work required is still sufficiently uncomplicated for all students to be able to gain some experience of achievement and success.

The foreign-language teacher usually starts off with a class with a set to learn. Lewin explains "set" as a tension in the nervous system which continues, and brings about action, until some goal is achieved which releases the tension.[10] If the teacher explains the aims and objectives of the foreign-language course and the methods to be employed to attain them, he may transform this attitude into a readiness to learn by a certain method.

Experiments have shown that the student will develop some kind of set toward the work, so this is the stage for the teacher to make explicit the approach required by the subject matter. "An active set to learn, with its accompanying selective process and active response to the material practiced, is a powerful determinant of learning. . . . The set may be established by formal instructions or may arise from . . . the subject's own reaction systems."[11]

In the audio-lingual method, it is particularly important to establish a co-operative attitude on the part of the students, or much of the repetitive practice may be a waste of time. It is well known that mere frequency of repetition without a set to learn does not result in efficient learning. Sanford reports having recited the prayers of the Episcopal service some five thousand times, at very regular intervals, in twenty-five years, and yet finding himself unable to recite them correctly on his own without prompting.[12]

By explaining the long road ahead, the teacher can also

---

[9] Harlow, Montgomery (Hilgard [1956], pp. 430–31), Woodworth, and Festinger (Woodworth [1958], pp. 77–79), among others, postulate a curiosity or exploratory drive. See also G. Blair, R. Jones, and R. Simpson, *Educational Psychology* (2d ed.; New York, 1962), pp. 176–78.

[10] Hilgard (1956), pp. 259–60, gives an account of Lewin's experiments on the set to reproduce.

[11] McGeoch and Irion (1952), p. 228.

[12] *Ibid.*, pp. 224–26.

obviate the effects of early disappointment at not being able to speak "like a native" after several weeks of study. Instead, students will experience a high degree of satisfaction from being able to speak a number of simple phrases "just like a native," while realizing that they are far from the ultimate goal. Marty, after long experience with the audio-lingual method, has decided that this motivation factor is the main contribution of the learning of dialogues.[13]

It is at this beginning stage that students who have had bitter experiences of failure in other subject areas for years may suddenly develop a great interest in foreign-language study, because here they are beginning on exactly the same level as everyone else, and the backlog of undigested principles and unperfected skills no longer counts against them. This new start inspires hope of continuing success, which is reinforcing to these students and so insures their persistence.

Those with poor aptitude for other scholastic work will find that the new subject provides many attainable short-term goals, with simple elements to be mastered, which act as incentives and lead to quick rewards for the effort expended.

There are students whose confidence in other subject areas has been blunted by embarrassment at making, before their classmates, what have appeared to be foolish responses based on lack of comprehension of previous learning; such students may overcome the inhibiting effect of anxiety by first making correct language responses aloud in group recitation and thus find it easier later to give a correct response alone. Success may give a new direction to the learned motivation of these students: they may develop a desire to learn for its own sake this language which has provided these rewarding new experiences, or at least a determination to work hard to remain in this class where such satisfactions are attainable.

To summarize, in a beginning foreign-language class there is a wide variety of individual motives energizing

---

[13] Marty (1963), p. vi.

the class members and determining the direction of their efforts. It is essential that the teacher be conscious of the individual character of motivation. As Mowrer says in his discussion of Lewin's field theory, "The effects of a given constellation of stimuli, a 'situation,' or a 'field,' upon an individual cannot be predicted or even understood without knowledge of the individual and what he *brings to* the situation."[14] In order to condition favorable attitudes[15] to the new subject, the teacher must be prompt in providing the rewarding experiences peculiar to each kind of motivation. Such favorable attitudes, frequently reinforced, can become so strong that they will persist despite the tedium which inevitably accompanies some of the work involved later in mastering the language. Experimentation has shown that when the incentive object is sufficiently attractive, people will willingly endure unattractive activity to attain the goal they have set themselves.[16]

If, however, the teacher is oblivious to the requirements of these individual motivations, they can become extinguished through accumulated inhibition due to the amount of work and effort required or be diverted into other channels as the work becomes more difficult. If the student's main interest has been the satisfaction of his curiosity about foreign language he will already be satisfied, and his efforts will cease through satiation rather than extinction. Early interest and enthusiasm must not be regarded as inevitably signifying interest in the language per se, although the ultimate development of such an interest is the aim of the foreign-language teacher.

The second function of motivation, according to Melton's analysis, is that of directing the variable and persistent activity of the organism. This aspect of motivation is of particular interest at the second stage, when the student comes to grips with the language in all its complexity. The motivation which energized him in the beginning stages has been replaced by other learned motivations, which may

---

[14] Mowrer (1960*a*), p. 309.
[15] Thus establishing a cathexis (Freud, Tolman) or positive valence (Lewin) for the foreign-language study.
[16] Woodworth and Schlosberg (1954), p. 661.

or may not be connected with persisting in the study of the foreign language. The curiosity drive has been satisfied; the reward of social approval (because he is studying a foreign language) has been experienced and no longer has a reinforcing influence. Certain elementary "requirements" have been fulfilled. The language study itself is now becoming much more demanding, with the possibility of fluent command still in the distant future. There are fewer short-term incentives. The student is expected to know and to be able to use a considerable body of learned material. At this stage, students tend to fall into three groups.

The student with little aptitude and poor powers of retention feels overwhelmed. As Mowrer would express it, the secondary reinforcement of hope (hope of becoming fluent in the language) has been withdrawn, without fulfillment, and the result is disappointment and hopelessness.[17] Such students are now motivated by a desire to avoid further anxiety and embarrassment, and this may lead to one of several forms of behavior. They may try to escape from the language class either actively by dropping the subject, symbolically by ceasing to learn their work and dropping so far behind the others that for all intents and purposes they are no longer with the group, or passively by ceasing to participate in active language work in the classroom, hoping in this way to escape notice and "sit it out" with the least possible embarrassment to themselves.

The second group of students has made satisfactory progress but is now losing interest. It is this second group that offers a puzzle to the teachers. Some of these students are well described in the Agard-Dunkel Investigation, where it was found that students "professed to be more highly motivated by oral-aural than by grammar and reading goals," but that their enthusiasm and interest began to wane as "the material became more and more difficult to assimilate."[18] Here, obviously, the attraction of the goal was not sufficiently strong to direct them in

---

[17] Mowrer (1960a), p. 164.
[18] Agard and Dunkel (1948), p. 292.

"persistent activity," especially as the oral-aural or audio-lingual method requires a great deal of persistent, repetitious activity which is not intrinsically interesting.

Not all the students who lose interest at this stage are discouraged by the increasing difficulty of the work, and yet they do not wish to continue their study of the language. Certain conclusions of the classical Gestalt school can help us to understand what has happened to this previously interested and enthusiastic group.

According to Koffka, one of the principles at work in the individual's reaction to his environment is a tendency toward "closure." "So long as an activity is incomplete, every new situation created by it is still . . . a transitional situation;" whereas when the individual has attained his goal "he has arrived at a situation which to him is an end-situation."[19] This end-situation is a state of minimal tension, and so, as McGeoch and Irion have stated, "once a motive is satisfied, the activity level declines."[20] This accords with Lewin's model, in which the attraction or valence of a goal creates a tension and maintains it until that goal is achieved. This attraction acts as a force which impels the individual to undertake certain activities leading to that goal. These activities may not be attractive in themselves, but the tension aroused by the greater attractiveness of the goal will enable the individual to persist in these activities as means to the end, until the goal (or the state of "closure") is reached.

If the student in the foreign-language class has been allowed to set himself, through ignorance of what is involved or through misleading information, a goal greatly inferior to mastery of the language, he will reach the state of closure during this second stage. He will feel satisfied with what he knows. Perhaps he is glib in handling memorized patterns and clichés of the foreign language. He may feel, then, that he knows enough to make himself understood as a tourist and fail altogether to comprehend

---

19 K. Koffka, *The Growth of the Mind* (1925), pp. 102–3, quoted in *Nebraska Symposium on Motivation* (Lincoln, 1960), ed. M. R. Jones, p. 147.
20 McGeoch and Irion (1952), p. 195.

the real depths of language mastery. For him, then, the study of the foreign language is finished, he loses interest, and his activity is directed into other channels by other motives.

Other members of this second group may not perceive themselves as achieving their goal at all. Such students may have been led to believe that certain new methods of study would enable them to acquire "near-native fluency" in record time, an idea which is all too current.[21] Not satisfied with the recitation of glib, if useful, phrases, these students feel that their perceived goal has not been reached in the time they had anticipated, and so they cease to make any further effort. Their motivation becomes extinguished through lack of perceived reward and is replaced by some more dominant motive which impels them to other activities.

The third group consists of those who, from the beginning, have been given a clear understanding of what it means to achieve mastery of a language, and who have perceived this as a long-term goal of sufficient worth to warrant long and persistent effort. These students have recognized certain subgoals as marks of progress: they have enjoyed the satisfaction of being able to read a simple story or play directly in the language without translating; they have felt pleasure at the insight they have gained into some aspects of a foreign culture or in being able to correspond with a student of similar age in the country where the language is spoken. Perhaps they have had the personal satisfaction of being able to act with facility a part in a foreign-language play, or they have discovered that they can follow the dialogue with reasonable ease when others are acting. Variety of activity in the foreign-language classroom is more likely to develop long-term motivation of this sort in the students by providing many opportunities to experience success and reward as they advance toward their goal.

Further insight into the extinction of energizing motivation at this second stage is given by some of the

---

[21] Many articles and advertisements in popular magazines have spread this idea in recent years. See advertisement quoted in chap. i.

experimental studies of Lambert and Gardner.[22] Lambert speaks of an "instrumental" orientation toward learning a foreign language, when the student is looking to his knowledge of the language to increase his skill for some future occupation, and an "integrative" orientation when the student desires to learn more about the cultural community of native speakers of the language, as if he desired to become identified with them. Experimental results (Gardner, 1960) have shown that the group with the integrative approach was more successful in foreign-language learning, particularly in developing skill in the active use of the language in communication. Students with the instrumental approach would fall into the third group, those who have found satisfaction in activities where they were approaching some stage of comprehension of and identification with the people of another culture. In view of the finding of Lambert and his associates (1962) that the majority of American foreign-language students are instrumentally oriented,[23] teachers in American schools, particularly, need to be alert to detect these differences of motivation if they wish to encourage students to go on to a stage of language mastery.

At the advanced level the student's motivation will determine which activities will be repeated and which eliminated. Some will drop the subject. Among these may be some that Lambert has warned us about in the results of another experiment: In advanced American students studying in Montreal who had reached the stage of "thinking in French," he found progressive development of feelings of "anomie," or social uncertainty and dissatisfaction, which developed as they lost some ties with their own cultural group and approached the stage of identity with a new group. These feelings made them seek opportunities to speak English, even though in this case it meant breaking a pledge to speak only French.[24] The teacher will need to watch for any signs of inner tension of this sort.

---

[22] Lambert (1963), Part II, pp. 114–18, gives a succinct account of these experiments.

[23] Lambert (1961), p. 157.

[24] Lambert (1963), Part II, p. 116. See also Lambert (1961), pp. 2–3.

Others will, however, choose to continue and develop a command of the language in all the skill areas (comprehension, speech, reading, and writing). Rewards at this stage are abundant and, as a result, foreign-language behavior is strongly reinforced. Many students become absorbed in foreign-language activity through student clubs, foreign films, the reading of foreign-language magazines of all types, modern plays, and novels. They converse in the foreign language whenever possible or appropriate, write letters and diaries in the language, and take an interest in the art and the music of the foreign people. These students advance rapidly on their own momentum, with the teacher as consultant and adviser.

The motive at this point has changed from the desire to learn the language to the desire to use the language as a native speaker would use it and to come to understand the people who speak it. These are obviously the students who are integratively oriented. Their motivation is intrinsic to the language itself, as the rich expression of another culture, and not extrinsic, in the sense that it can be used for their own purposes like any other tool. The teacher must aim at developing this type of intrinsic motivation in as many of his students as possible for the earliest stages of foreign-language study.

PART II: EMOTIONAL ASPECTS OF FOREIGN-LANGUAGE LEARNING

If the student is to be induced to behave, there is another type of reaction to be taken into account, that dominated by his emotions. Mowrer considers that "the emotions are of quite extraordinary importance in the total economy of living organisms."[1] His view that "we are constantly trying to get from 'regions' of emotional tension to 'regions' of emotional comfort"[2] is supported by the research of Lewin and the pleasure principle of Freud. That

---

[1] Mowrer (1960a), p. 308.
[2] Ibid., p. 274.

emotion plays an important part in the learning of the native language has already been pointed out in chapter iv, and the position will now be taken that it plays an equally important part in foreign-language learning.

It is well to examine the demands made of the student learning a foreign language. We are asking him to return to a very immature stage in his development. Much of his ability to adjust to the environment and to manipulate people and materials has come with his increasing skill in the use of his native language. It has taken him many years (thirteen or fourteen if he is an adolescent) to achieve this control of his own language as an effective tool, almost an arm of his personality. Suddenly he is plunged back into complete helplessness. Over long years he has been taught to leave behind immature ways; he has been conditioned by the approval and disapproval of elders and peers to be ashamed of behaving like an infant. Now he is asked to do just that; to practice strange sounds, to fumble about with strange words and modes of expression, to follow blindly the lead of the teacher, and to lay aside his well-trained habits of thinking for himself. The material he is asked to learn or read often has a childish content, so that he feels ridiculous repeating it. He is also in danger of making foolish mistakes in a public situation, with the possibility of his companions laughing at him. In other classes he is rewarded for showing originality and initiative, but in the foreign-language class he must not do this under any circumstances. He must only imitate, limiting what he has to express to·the few simple ideas for which he has learned the foreign expressions. As Sanford has pointed out, "There are many indications that language is a vehicle of personality as well as of thought, for when the person speaks, he tells not only about the world but also, through both form and content, about himself."[3] The student of the second language cannot yet do this. When he tries to express what he is really thinking, he lapses into the modes of expression of his own language and is rebuked. He must think and

---

[3] E. Sanford, "Speech and Personality," *Psychological Bulletin*, XXXIX, 840 (quoted in Carroll [1953], p. 79).

talk for a while in an unreal world where you say not what you want to say but only what can be concocted from the few foreign-language forms you know, no matter how infantile or how irrelevant to real-life affairs it may seem. Undoubtedly, facts like these were behind Nida's observation, from case studies, that some intelligent missionary students found the learning of a foreign language difficult because of "their conception (perhaps unconscious) that to learn the language would be to risk a loss of face (e.g., 'making a fool of oneself') or more general prestige."[4] For the same reasons, tourists who have learned at school the language of the country they are visiting are often hesitant about uttering their first phrases in the presence of native speakers of the language.

Here is fertile ground for frustration, anxiety, embarrassment, humiliation, and their associated emotional states. Unless the teacher realizes this initial disadvantage on the part of the student, he can cause a great distaste for foreign-language learning because of its association with unpleasant emotional excitement.

Emotional responses such as anxiety are considered to be learned, through the association of a previously neutral stimulus-situation with aversive experiences.[5] These situations then become capable of arousing strong emotion in themselves. These unpleasant emotions act as motivating forces, but they have a disruptive effect upon behavior when they become very intense. Anxiety, for instance, can act as a drive or motivating force which will stimulate the student to greater efforts in the attempt to gain reassurance or to reduce anxiety; similarly, humiliation can drive the student to improve his work in order to escape from the embarrassment associated with it. But when these unpleasant drives become intense, their full emotional effect becomes very disturbing and may express itself in various ways. The student may, for instance, seek escape in passivity, refusing to utter foreign-language sounds aloud, and, in extreme cases, making only per-

---

[4] Pimsleur, Mosberg, and Morrison, "Student Factors in Foreign Language Learning," p. 17, in Pimsleur (1961).

[5] Keller and Schoenfeld (1950), pp. 329–42.

functory efforts to learn anything associated with the foreign language. On the other hand, he may show antagonism, which sometimes finds expression in an aggressive return to an "American accent" and a deliberate use of native-language patterns in the foreign language.[6] In this way he regains a sense of security. Such behavior is reinforced by escape from the anxiety, frustration, or humiliation of oral expression in the foreign language, and also, in cases where some classmates share these feelings, by the approval of these other students whose esteem is valued more than that of the teacher.

Excessive drive or emotional disturbance can also fixate behavior, so that, although the student is most anxious to please the teacher or improve his efforts, he finds himself repeating the same mistakes. The harder he tries, the less able he is to distinguish the way in which his response differs from the required response. Finally, he takes refuge in stereotyped behavior and learning is inhibited.[7] This is particularly likely to occur in foreign-language learning, because the student is dependent on others for the correct form of behavior and begins to feel hopeless and inadequate when he cannot work his way out of his difficulties by his own efforts. It is also frequent with students who cannot distinguish nuances of sound, either because of structural differences of the ear or because they are eye-minded rather than ear-minded and feel insecure when forced to depend on hearing alone. The more anxious they become, the less accurately can they discriminate. Short phrases are recognized briefly, then rapidly slip out of their minds. Their panic increases until finally all they can hear is something approximating what communications engineers call "white noise."[8] Everything is an auditory blur, and they are unable to distinguish separate tones. This frustration and increasing

---

[6] Mowrer terms these two reactions passive and active avoidance behavior: Mowrer (1960a), p. 33.

[7] McGeoch and Irion (1952), p. 208.

[8] "White noise" is random noise, compounded of all frequencies of vibration in equal amounts. It gives a "hishing" sound which prevents one from distinguishing separate tones. See G. Miller (1951), pp. 54–55.

tension make a negatively valenced barrier of the spoken language, to use Lewinian terms, and as a result the student tends either to resent the audio-lingual emphasis of the course or to "leave the field" (give up trying as soon as work is presented orally). The teacher must be alert to recognize when these types of difficulties are due to emotional disturbances and be ready to set the student at his ease, to distract attention from him, and to engage him in some relaxing activity which will restore his confidence.

A situation of this kind may be complicated even further by a conflict between a strong desire to learn the language, for professional, social, or personal reasons (creating a positive valence for the foreign-language goal), and a strong aversion to the oral work associated with it (giving this a negative valence). This situation can be alleviated to some extent if there is a balance between oral and visual activity in the foreign-language class. This is one of the arguments in favor of introducing reading, and some controlled writing, into the foreign-language lesson much sooner than some advocates of the audio-lingual method would allow. In their report on five years' experience with French in the elementary school at the University of Chicago Laboratory School, Dunkel and Pillet state that they had to introduce reading into their program earlier than they had planned, because it provided "a new medium for any students having difficulty with the audio-lingual approach." They also found that the introduction of formal grammatical study "offered another approach to some students who had not done well through the audio-lingual approach and thus gave them another opportunity to salvage something from their language experience."[9]

The high-school teacher of foreign-languages deals with students of all kinds of abilities, motivations, and emotional reactions. If he wishes to "induce" each one of them to "behave" in the language, he must see that the methods he employs are sufficiently varied to provide for their indi-

---

[9] Dunkel and Pillet (1962), pp. 46–49.

vidual learning needs. In this way, despite any emotional inhibitions, each student will have the opportunity for some beneficial contact with the foreign language and culture. It is true that all normal children learn their native language in a similar way, but, even in a situation completely different from the foreign-language classroom and with much more intense motivation, they still learn it to varying degrees of proficiency and over widely varying periods of time. It is inevitable that similar differences in verbal ability will become evident in the foreign-language class, and the experience of Dunkel and Pillet was that "these differences persist and tend to increase in magnitude."[10] What may appear theoretically to be the "best" or most effective way of teaching a foreign language may well bar some members of the class from sharing in the foreign-language experience through emotional stress. To avoid such a possibility, methods should be as varied as the diversity of the class demands.

It is clear from the situations described in this chapter that there is a strong emotional element involved in the learning of a foreign language, just as there is in the learning of the native language. The small child needs the security and encouragement of a warm and loving atmosphere in order to develop verbal fluency, and the student of the foreign language needs to feel at ease with his teacher if he is to be able to imitate and assimilate the language adequately. (This is, incidentally, an element which is completely lacking in a language laboratory booth, unless it is supplied by the supervising teacher.) In a recent analysis of the factors involved in foreign-language learning ability, Pimsleur, Stockwell, and Comrey emphasized this aspect. They concluded that in establishing adequate criterion tests for achievement in oral-aural skills entirely new factors will have to be included, and that "among such new factors, the personality of the student and the characteristics of the teacher are those which appear most promising and are most in need of research attention."[11]

With the audio-lingual method, the characteristics and personality of the teacher become much more important

---

[10] *Ibid.*, p. 60.
[11] Pimsleur *et al.* (1961), report No. 2, p. 19.

than with a grammar-translation or reading approach. The student is asked to imitate as exactly as possible the intonation, tone of voice, even the gestures, of the teacher. If the student dislikes the teacher or feels ill at ease with him, then the student is reluctant to identify himself with the teacher to this degree. The teacher must understand the interplay of personalities within the class group. The student may be willing to imitate the teacher accurately but be unwilling to make himself conspicuous among his classmates by the excellence of his performance. Because of the acquired motivation in our society to conform, he may prefer to tone down his accent and intonation to the average of his group. Further, if the teacher is a perfectionist and tends to be too critical of every small mistake, the group or the individual student may perceive the task as an impossible one, and this may arouse tension and aggressive reactions which tend to fixate the incorrect responses. This is particularly likely in the area of pronunciation. The teacher must realize the difficulty the student will have in changing physical habits which have become automatic over a long period of native-language use. Many teachers tend to forget that the child learns to discriminate correct sounds that he hears in his native language long before he is able to use them correctly himself, and that he is often five or six years old before the last incorrect pronunciations are eliminated from his speech. It is only by the patient rewarding of successive approximations, without embarrassment or harassment, that the teacher can gradually lead the student to a near-native pronunciation.

An interesting experiment which clearly supports the position taken in this chapter is reported by Charles Curran of Loyola University, Chicago.[12] Students were taught four European languages in special group conversation sessions by instructors trained in counseling skills. All four of the languages were spoken in the same conversation group, but each student concentrated on expressing himself in one of the languages. One aim of the research was "to study the

---

[12] C. A. Curran, "Counseling Skills Adapted to the Learning of Foreign Languages," *Bulletin of the Menninger Clinic*, XXV, No. 2 (March, 1961), 78–93.

subtleties of the relationship between the language expert
and the learner, particularly those factors that decreased
the learner's sense of threat, insecurity and anxiety and
furthered his sense of trust, belonging and identification
with and security in the relationship with the language
expert." The experiment showed clearly that the students
began the experience with a sense of threat; conflict, confusion, and a feeling of inadequacy predominated. Their
growth toward confidence and independence in foreign-
language activity was found to depend on the degree of
warmth, acceptance, and empathy that the counselor-in-
structor was able to convey. Group members had begun
to feel secure with their counselors long before they ceased
to feel insecure and threatened by each other in foreign-
language communication, but they became more confident
and reassured as they realized that each other member of
the group had the same personal struggles and anxieties
that they had. The study concluded that, "as in psychological
counseling, the client's growth was most effectively furthered when there was an intense empathy between himself
and the language counselor. Through this he could slowly
grow in a more independent understanding of and coping
with his language problems. He could thus grow in language
maturity and responsible independence."

The circumstances of this experiment were more dramatic
than those of the usual classroom, in that four languages
were used in the same group sessions. Undoubtedly, the
emotional reactions were more marked because of this. The
same emotions and problems are nevertheless encountered
in a less intense form wherever foreign-language learning
takes place in a group situation, and the findings provide
valuable food for thought for the high-school teacher.

This examination of the problems awaiting the teacher
in the area of oral work indicates that his role in inducing
the student to behave in the language is to do all he can to
avoid discouraging or upsetting the student. This is a negative approach. With foreknowledge of the pitfalls, the
teacher's role is rather to use his understanding of motivational forces to increase the student's enthusiasm and desire
to express himself in the language. McClelland has empha-

sized this aspect of motivation, defining a motive as "a strong affective association characterized by an anticipatory goal reaction and based on past association with pleasure or pain."[13] He feels that a drive-reduction theory emphasizes only the negative side of motivation, and that the positive affective aspect is equally important. We seek pleasant experiences because we enjoy the quality of experience they bring. "*Slight* changes in intensity of stimulation tend to arouse pleasant affect, *extreme* changes unpleasant affect."[14] With this in mind, the teacher should see that the experiences he directs in the foreign-language class give to the study of the language pleasant associations which will carry the student over the dull periods which must come from time to time as the work becomes harder and more demanding. Only in this way can he hope to "induce the student to behave" in the language as he needs to do if he is to reach the stage of language mastery.

---

[13] Quoted in Hilgard (1956), p. 432.
[14] *Ibid.*, p. 433.

X

ASSUMPTION 2

LANGUAGE SKILLS ARE LEARNED MORE EFFEC-
TIVELY IF ITEMS OF THE FOREIGN LANGUAGE
ARE PRESENTED IN SPOKEN FORM
BEFORE WRITTEN FORM

THE MOTTO "Listening-Speaking-Reading-Writing" on the Audio-Lingual Materials does not reflect a completely original approach to foreign-language teaching. At a UNESCO seminar in Ceylon in 1953, attended by foreign-language teachers from nineteen nations, agreement was reached that the order of teaching the four fundamental skills of a foreign language should be understanding, speaking, reading, and writing.[1] This is consistent with the viewpoint of the linguistic scientists in the Bloomfield tradition that language is primarily "a system of arbitrary vocal symbols of experience," while the written language is "a symbolization of a symbolization, a reminding system of something said or that might have been said."[2] This stress on language as vocal behavior is appropriate to our present experience of a shrinking world. People who never dreamed that they would meet and work with speakers of other tongues are finding themselves on missions abroad or working side by side in laboratory and workshop with such people. In these circumstances, hearing and speaking the language acquire much more relevance than reading or writing it. Yet, in an earlier

---

[1] UNESCO, *The Teaching of Modern Languages* (Paris, 1955), p. 50.

[2] Parker (1962), p. 73.

era, proficiency in reading the foreign language seemed in many areas the most reasonable objective for which to work in the classroom, the written word being the closest probable contact the student would ever have with the language. The oral-aural approach, with its greater relevance for the modern age, has become more practicable with the development of mechanical aids such as tape-recorders, language laboratories, and television, which make it possible for the highly motivated student to practice for long hours without the physical presence of a teacher. The teacher can thus extend his influence without the tremendous expenditure of energy which once exhausted even the most enthusiastic teachers long before the students had had sufficient oral practice.

The aim of this portion of the study, however, is not to examine changing objectives but to see what psychological factors are involved in this suggested order of foreign-language learning, particularly as it is advocated methodologically by the proponents of the audio-lingual method.

The major argument in the sources is that as the development of skills in the order: listening, speaking, reading, writing, is the "natural" or "proper" order for learning a second language,[3] the ear and tongue should be trained first without the support of the written language,[4] and the student should not, in the early stages, read anything he has not already learned to understand and say.[5] The term "early stages" is ill-defined. Brooks says this should also be the practice at later stages.[6] He proposes "a sustained experience (of weeks or even months) in listening and speaking" to precede training in reading, and then a further period when only what has been heard and repeated should be read.[7]

The use of the expression "natural order" shows that here the advocates of this method are basing their argument on the way the child learns his native language. It is ob-

[3] Northeast Conference (1961), p. 43; NEA (1960), p. 20.
[4] NEA (1960), p. 20; Politzer (1961), p. 69; Brooks (1960), p. 107.
[5] Northeast Conference (1961), p. 18; NEA (1960), p. 20; Brooks (1960), p. 123; Politzer (1961), p. 8.
[6] Northeast Conference (1961), p. 18.
[7] Brooks (1960), p. 123.

vious, without any profound study of child development, that this was the order of native-language learning. This, however, is not of itself an incontrovertible reason for adopting the same order for learning a foreign language, unless it can be shown that the situation in both cases is sufficiently similar to warrant such a conclusion.

Without going over the well-traversed ground of how a child learns his mother tongue,[8] we may note immediately some similarities and several clear distinctions between this situation and that of the student learning a foreign language in a high-school classroom.

The first and most obvious difference is that the infant learning his native language is at the same time discovering the possibilities of his own organs and exploring his environment. So, for the infant, physical maturation, the formation of concepts, and the development of the forms of speech of his community are taking place simultaneously. It is obvious that for him hearing must precede speaking, because what he eventually speaks will be the learned imitation of the arbitrary symbols of the language of the people who are nurturing him—the language by which he is surrounded in his home. It is equally obvious that he is dependent on what he hears, because he has not yet learned to read. The high-school student, on the other hand, has learned to control his speech organs in a certain way and has great difficulty in learning new speech habits. He has already formed concepts about his environment, which, for the most part, conform to the concepts of those about him and are embodied in the language which he has learned to speak. He has learned this language so well that it comes automatically to his lips when he wishes to communicate, and so interferes with his efforts to express himself in a new language. He is not surrounded by people speaking the foreign language and so does not hear it continually, as

---

[8] This subject is discussed very thoroughly in the following books: M. M. Lewis, *How Children Learn To Speak* (1957) and *Infant Speech* (1936); Dorothea McCarthy, "Language Development in Children" in L. Carmichael (ed.), *Manual of Child Psychology* (1946); W. Leopold, *Speech Development of a Bilingual Child: A Linguist's Record* (1949). G. Miller, *Language and Communication* (1951), chap. vii; and H. Dunkel, *Second-Language Learning* (1948), chap. ii.

he heard his native language. He has been to school for six, seven, or eight years and has learned to read, to study, and to extract much valuable information from books. His situation is therefore in many ways different from that of the infant. Whereas the infant has many hours a day for many years in which to learn his native language slowly and steadily, the high-school student has at best two hours a day for five days of the week and is expected to make fast progress.

The child begins with simple words which act as complete sentences (holophrases). He names things incorrectly while forming categories, mispronounces words (sometimes for years), and makes the best approximation he can to the sounds he hears about him, and all this is considered "cute." The family even takes his baby words into its repertoire and speaks to him in imitation of his own language. He is expected to take these fumbling steps and is richly rewarded for the efforts he makes, inaccurate though his imitations may be. Slowly and unsteadily, without analytic explanations, he achieves control of a most complex grammatical system. On the other hand, in the audio-lingual method, the student is expected to learn complete sentences of complicated grammatical structure from the very beginning.[9] He must repeat these accurately and pronounce them as correctly as possible with newly learned positions of the speech organs. He must not, as the infant does, experiment with new combinations and analogies, some accurate and some inaccurate. Instead he must be induced to produce the right response by the teacher's careful arrangement of the circumstances of response. His mistakes are not "cute" but dangerous, in that they represent decremental, not incremental, learning.

The infant has a tremendous desire to communicate. He has needs he wants supplied. He is anxious to gain the attention and share in the activities of those around him. As Miller and Dollard have said, "The child learns to talk

---

[9] In *French*, Level One, Unit 1, of the A-L M materials we find "Comment s'appelle-t-il" and "Allons-y," and in Unit 2, "Il faut que j'aille chercher un livre," none of which can be considered similar in structural difficulty to the holophrases of the infant.

because society makes that relatively effortless response supremely worthwhile."[10] The high-school student, on the other hand, as has already been pointed out, must limit and restrict himself. His efforts at communication in the foreign language are frequently thwarted by his lack of knowledge, and he must be willing to return in spirit and in production to an earlier stage of learning. It is true that he has other motives to spur him on—desire to learn another language or to have it at his command as a tool, desire to please parents or teachers, or eagerness to achieve good grades—but these do not have the compelling force of the child's more primitive motivation.

The two situations being so dissimilar, it seems unreasonable to derive methods of foreign-language learning from the way the child learns his native language. The temptation, however, is great. Most writers, while acknowledging the great differences in the two situations, manage to slip in a few recommendations based on native-language learning while their readers are off their guard and present them as cogent arguments for certain procedures. This is the technique that is employed in support of training the ear and the tongue without the support of the eye. If this reasoning is accepted as valid in this case, then, for the sake of consistency, other aspects of infant learning must be accepted as well—the slow and tortuous acquisition of words, used first in a generalized sense and acquiring specific reference later; the use of single words with the force of phrases; the use of simple phrases with incorrect pronoun forms or verb agreements; inaccurate pronunciations repeated over many weeks. These aspects of child learning are, however, rejected without a second thought.

A perfectly legitimate case can be established for the order: hearing, speaking, reading, writing, without resort to such unwarranted derivation from infant learning. Because the foreign language is a set of arbitrary symbols adopted by a certain community, with an arbitrary standard of acceptable pronunciation, it is obvious that the student

---

[10] Miller and Dollard (1941), p. 82.

should hear it correctly before endeavoring to reproduce it. It is equally obvious that he cannot learn it accurately from a script with which he has always associated his own speech sounds, unless an initiate unlocks for him the secrets of the new sound associations. Having seen what are the conventional ways of writing this new code, he can then attempt to write it himself. Let us see whether an equally reasonable case can be made out for training the ear and the tongue without the support of the eye.

If the speaking objective is to be given first priority, then, according to Guthrie, we should practice in the precise form which we wish the student to use later. We should discover the cues which lead to this type of behavior and arrange the situation with as many stimulus supports as possible, so that the behavior will occur.[11] This is consistent with Mowrer's concept of response-correlated stimuli. If we wish the student to speak (and to understand), then the stimuli associated with these responses must have been associated a number of times with successful experiences and thus be conditioned to the emotion of hope. In this way, the student will feel hope when these stimuli are presented (or, in the case of response-correlated stimuli, experienced) and will repeat the behavior which was previously rewarded. If the student's successful experiences have been associated with written work alone, these stimuli will be absent in a conversational situation; the student will experience disappointment or anxiety, depending on which of these has been conditioned to the speaking situation, and so the response of understanding the spoken word or replying in the foreign language will not be easily forthcoming. For the development of facility in understanding and speaking, there must be much practice in these skills with success and enjoyment.

That the development of this ready response in understanding and speaking will be hindered if the student is trained with the spoken word supported by the written notation of what he is saying is not, however, easy to maintain when we consider carefully the results of research in sensory perception.

---

[11] Hilgard (1956), p. 64.

Objection has been made to a method which limits presentation of material to the ear only on the ground that people learn more rapidly from visual than from aural materials. Research evidence for this is not conclusive. Underwood, summarizing the results of the experimentation in this area, says, "The superiority of one method over the other, when found, has not been great and seems to be largely a function of the S's (subject's) previous experience."[12] At the high-school level this experience, as far as school work is concerned, comes largely from books, or with the support of visual materials. In our culture, the ability to listen, comprehend, and retain material heard but not seen has not been developed. As Carroll suggests, "manipulating auditory materials without visual support is possibly a process which can be learned,"[13] but, while it is being learned, one must expect a certain amount of failure and tension on the part of the students. One of the tasks of the foreign-language teacher is to develop this ability, but, while it is being developed, access to a written notation for verification and aid in recall will relieve the tension of many students and so enable them to concentrate their energies on acquiring the new skill. As their confidence increases, they will need this support less and less.

The strongest argument in favor of some visual support for the aural presentation of the foreign language in the early stages comes, however, from studies of organization in perception rather than from studies of the relative effectiveness of different sense modalities in learning. We must consider seriously the question, what are we asking the student to grasp in our aural presentation? In our own language, our understanding of what is aurally presented is largely guided by well-established word associations, familiar syntactic structures which lead us to expect certain classes of words in certain positions, so that if we do not hear clearly we can frequently supply what is missing from the cues given by the context. The student learning a foreign language finds himself, especially in the early stages,

---

[12] B. Underwood, *Experimental Psychology, an Introduction* (New York, 1949), p. 419.
[13] Carroll (1960), p. 45.

completely bereft of such supports. He has to hear everything, and hear it clearly. He has also to retain everything,
if he is to learn the aural material presented. If he is
intellectually capable and highly motivated, he will take all
this in his stride; but if he is uncertain of himself, anxious,
has poor auditory discrimination, or indifferent powers of retention, what he has to learn passes in the air, and he has
no support to which to turn to give him a further chance to
grasp what he has not understood. Much of his puzzlement
is due to his inability to retain strange sounds in unac-
customed groupings long enough to rehearse them again
subvocally and so strengthen the memory trace. The slight-
est wavering of attention through distraction, mental fatigue, or satiation means that he has lost something which
he cannot hear again without the co-operation of another
person.

From research on perception, Hebb has drawn the conclusion that there are three kinds of perceptual unity.[14]
The first is the primitive unity of a figure as distinct from
its background, which, so far as is known, is distinguished
by all creatures. The second is a "non-sensory figure-ground
organization," where the boundaries of the figure are not
fixed by physical elements of sight but are affected by experience. Thus, we may see in a figure something which
other people do not see, and yet on another occasion we may
not see the same thing at all. Here there is an interplay between the primary and the non-sensory unity. The third
kind of unity is "identity," which is "defined . . . as referring to the properties of association inherent in a perception."[15] In this case, a figure is seen as falling into a certain
category, that is, as being similar or dissimilar to other
figures. "The object that is perceived as having identity is
capable of being associated readily with other objects or
with some action, whereas the one that does not have identity is recalled with great difficulty or not at all, and is not
recognized or named easily."

Research in the perception of speech reported by G.

---

[14] D. Hebb, *The Organization of Behavior* (New York, 1949), pp.
19–35.
[15] *Ibid.*, p. 26.

Miller[16] shows clearly that the same three kinds of perceptual unity apply in this area. The person listening to a strange language for the first time hears it as detached from the background noise around him. This is the primitive unity of auditory perception. Because of his general experience with his native language, he soon perceives it as more than noise distinct from other noises. He detects a certain rhythm in the flow and a musical rise and fall of the voice. This parallels the non-sensory unity described by Hebb. The stage of "identity," however, where the hearer can distinguish the pattern in what he is hearing, associate it with other patterns or with active responses, and recall it with ease, comes as the result of a much more complicated process than that involved in mere hearing. To understand what is involved in this third stage, we turn to communications research. Communications engineers, in dealing with problems in sending telegraphic messages, have brought out a number of elements in the perception of speech which are relevant to this question of "identity."

"Information," as used in communications studies,[17] refers to the range of possible alternative words which could occur in a certain position in speech. The amount of "information" a particular word conveys is therefore a function of the number of possible alternatives which would be meaningful to us in that position. The amount of information we can derive from hearing an utterance is increased by certain factors which reduce the number of possible alternatives: the tendency in the native language to use certain sequences of sounds and not others, familiar sequences of words, the syntactic rules which limit the occurrence of certain words in certain positions in the utterance, and the frame of expectations which surrounds the utterance, these expectations being derived from the total situation in which the utterance takes place. All of these factors depend on the

---

[16] G. Miller (1951), chap. iii; Licklider and Miller, "The Perception of Speech," in S. S. Stevens (ed.), *Handbook of Experimental Psychology* (New York, 1951).

[17] See C. Hockett's review of *The Mathematical Theory of Communications*, by C. Shannon and W. Weaver, in *Saporta* (1961), pp. 44–67.

acuity of one individual's auditory discrimination. Miller states that "the information we convey is coded into a pattern of words. The relations among the components of the patterns must be known before the individual components can be decoded."[18] In an ordinary native-language situation, it is a well-known fact that we do not need to hear everything that is said in order to understand. We have all experienced this phenomenon when listening to sound films, taking part in a conversation in a crowded room or against a background of noise, or hearing scraps of conversation from a distance. Because of these factors of redundancy in speech, and our knowledge of them from previous experience, "the ear is very facile in patching together interrupted fragments of speech and reconstructing the whole message from only half the original wave form."[19] Here, too, the stage of "identity" in perception is shown to be the result of past associations and considerable experience. One of the commonest phrases among children in the earlier stages of association with the native language is "Whadyusay?" (or "Huh?"), because experience has been insufficient to enable them to piece together the elements of an utterance they have heard and deduce from these the total utterance.

These elements of "information" which help us to "identify" what we hear closely parallel Fries's "modes of meaning."[20] According to Fries, "linguistic meaning . . . consists of lexical meanings within a frame of structural meanings." The lexical items we hear are identified not only by contrastive patterns of sound sequences, but also by the distribution of each lexical item with sets of other lexical items with which we are accustomed to hearing them associated. Structural meaning is signaled by the "contrastive features of arrangement in which the lexical items occur." To these is added "social-cultural meaning," acquired through our day-to-day experiences, which to a large extent determines our reaction to what we hear.

A few minutes' thought will show the relevance of these

---

[18] G. Miller (1951), p. 113.
[19] *Ibid.*, p. 71.
[20] C. C. Fries, "Meaning and Linguistic Analysis," in *Language,* XXX (1954), 57–68.

facts about the perception of speech to the foreign-language learning situation. As initiates familiar with the foreign language, teachers tend to expect a degree of accuracy and completeness in auditory perception from students which they do not even possess in the native language, and which depends upon the discrimination of language cues (familiar sequences of sounds and words, syntactic relationships) which the student has not yet had sufficient experience of the foreign language to acquire. Hill sums up this situation succinctly in his discussion of the linguistic level of meaning. "The native hearer," he says, "is trained to make full use of partially predictable items and sequences," and so can understand even mumbled and slurred utterances. "Our difficulty in understanding a foreign tongue . . . is largely that we do not make full use of partial predictability. We cannot, in other words, make use of prediction to reconstruct a partially heard sentence or to recognize which of two possible interpretations is the more probable."[21]

There are several stages of preparation necessary before students can be expected to identify clearly what they hear. First, as Miller has pointed out, "If a listener is completely unprepared for the sequence of speech sounds that he hears his ability to mimic the sounds is greatly reduced."[22] This provides a cogent argument for a period of training in the discrimination of the sounds of the foreign language, as advocated by some proponents of the audio-lingual method, before the student can be expected to mimic complete utterances. These sounds should be presented in complete words so that the student acquires at the same time experience with the acceptable sequences of sounds in that language. Training should be given not only in contrasting native sounds with apparently similar foreign-language sounds but also in contrasting close, but phonemically distinct, sounds in the new language.

Familiar sequences of sounds are only one factor in the redundancy of information in an utterance; there is the

---

[21] A. A. Hill, *Introduction to Linguistic Structures* (New York, 1958), p. 416.
[22] G. Miller (1951), p. 79.

other important factor of syntactic organization. This is completely lacking as a cue in the early stages of association with a foreign language. In the foreign languages commonly taught in high schools, as in English, the words fall into classes, each with its essential function. These functional relationships form a stable framework which is a guide to comprehension. It is the contention of the writer that the beginning student left to draw these out of the air in a completely aural situation is put in a difficult position. He is trying to acquire the discriminations necessary to distinguish word groups from the whole pattern of speech, and he is asked at the same time to make much finer distinctions within these groups, which it is possible he does not hear at all clearly. However, if some of the material is presented in written form, he is able to study it at his leisure, to examine its construction, and to organize what he is hearing and repeating. "Perceiving speech is not a passive, automatic procedure. The perceiver contributes a selective function by responding to some aspects of the total situation and not to others. He responds to the stimuli according to some organization that he imposes upon them. And he supplements the inconsistent or absent stimulation in a manner that is consistent with his needs and his past experience."[23] If the teacher does not help the student to create this organization which he imposes upon the fleeting sounds of the foreign language, the student will impose some form of his own to which the teacher has no access and which he cannot therefore correct if necessary. The objection that the orthography of the foreign language will arouse native-language associations and so lead to interference from native-language pronunciations is perfectly valid, but this interference can be overcome by intensive and continuous training in the association of foreign-language sounds with their written forms, a process which will have to take place sooner or later.

Differential reinforcement of the correct association of sound and symbol will lead to the gradual extinction of the unacceptable association. This method follows Guthrie's

---

[23] *Ibid.*, p. 79.

recommendation for breaking up a habit, namely, that the teacher should cause other movements to occur in the presence of the cues to the habit.[24] By training the student to pronounce the foreign words correctly in the presence of the written or printed script, the teacher is associating desirable responses with the cues previously associated with native-language sounds only. In the future, then, when the student has a set to read the foreign language from the written symbols, he will produce the foreign-language sounds in response to the cues. Most persistent attention will need to be given to the pronunciation of words which are spelled the same way in the two languages, as inter-ference is always greatest when similarity of stimuli is greatest. There will be periods of spontaneous recovery of the interfering association, but these will become fewer as the desired association becomes stronger.

This interference problem with the written script will have to be faced at some stage. In *Language Laboratory Learning,* Marty discusses his experiments, at Middlebury and elsewhere, in varying the length of the time lag between oral study of foreign-language material and its presenta-tion in written form. "All our experiments," he says, "clearly indicate that *no matter how long or how short the time lag* the introduction of the spelling presents the same *potential* danger. The students with superior or good lin-guistic ability usually avoid this danger; *no matter how long or how short the time lag,* they learn to spell without difficulty and without endangering their speech habits. . . . The students with mediocre or poor linguistic ability . . . find that their speech habits are constantly threatened by the spelling they are learning. . . . Thus, in spite of many articles to the contrary, we have found that a long time lag does not produce better audio-oral results than a short one. A further danger of a long time lag is that correct spelling habits are often delayed. During the strictly audio-oral period, it is nearly impossible to stop our high school and college students from devising their "own" phonetic spell-ing. . . . Even if you could stop them from writing, you

---

24 Hilgard (1956), p. 56.

could not stop them from seeing these spellings in their minds. The longer the time lag, the more strongly these spellings become fixed and the more difficult it is to eradicate them. . . . What really matters is not the length of the time lag, but the vigilance of the teacher."[25]

If the teacher is conscious of the dangers of interference of native-language habits, he can take the necessary steps to obviate them, always realizing the necessity for unremitting vigilance in this regard. The advantages in the greater assurance with which many students will approach their oral work and mimicry after they have been given some opportunity to see in written form what they are to practice seem to outweigh these rectifiable disadvantages. Introduction to the written form of the language should be made very early in the study of the language, so that training in the new association may be as prolonged as possible. This does not mean the introduction of new materials for reading in the early stages, but rather the presentation in written form of the limited materials which are being practiced orally.

Students have varied capacities and degrees of perceptual skill. The written script is of incalculable help to students with poor auditory discrimination; such students have enough tensions induced by the formidable nature of their task of understanding clearly and repeating acceptably sounds which they have the greatest difficulty in hearing distinctly, without the added insecurity of finding themselves completely dependent on their fallible ears for the material they must learn. Dunkel and Pillet, in their report on experiences at the Laboratory School of the University of Chicago, point out what a help the printed word was to students in their classes who were having difficulty with the audio-lingual approach.[26] Such students can often use their knowledge of structure and vocabulary, acquired from the written script, to piece together the information they do get from what they hear, and so arrive at an understanding similar to that which one gets in the native language in a "noisy" situation. The written script also gives students

---

[25] F. Marty, *Language Laboratory Learning* (Wellesley, Mass., 1960), pp. 75–76.
[26] Dunkel and Pillet (1962), pp. 45–48.

a tangible aid to memory and so decreases their dependence on the teacher or the tape.

The greatest safeguard against interference or negative transfer from the native language is not to keep the student from access to the written word, but to put into effect the last recommendation of the audio-lingual group set out above; namely, that in the early stages the student should not see anything in writing that he has not already heard or said. We may qualify this by adding, "or that he is not simultaneously hearing," and thereby associating sound and symbol. Later, when this interference is less, and when his knowledge of the foreign-language patterns is sufficient for him to read fluently without feeling the necessity to seek native-language equivalents for what he is reading, he should be encouraged to read more widely, and so to increase his knowledge of the language, without depending entirely on what the teacher supplies.

This support of the written word does not mean that the student should not receive much training in listening to the foreign language without a written script, nor does it mean that the first presentation of new material may not be in oral form with books closed. It does mean that the student should be allowed to see the work which he is to learn by heart and be drilled in associating foreign-language sound with foreign-language script immediately after the first oral presentation of the work, before continuing with further oral drill unsupported by the graphic symbol. The student should also be allowed access to this visual memory stimulus when the teacher is not at his side to help him with recall. In this way he will reach the stage of "identity" in perception much more rapidly as he organizes what he is hearing. It is in the early stages that he has greatest need of this support. Later, when he has a clear idea of the general organization of the language structure, he will find it much easier to identify and therefore retain what he has encountered purely in the oral form.

As Ferdinand de Saussure has said, "Writing . . . is used continually to represent language. We cannot simply disregard it. We must be acquainted with its usefulness, shortcomings, and dangers."[27] There is no reason why this should

---

[27] Saussure (1959), p. 23.

not be as true in the early stages of learning a language as in the later stages, so long as the written script is regarded merely as a help to memory and understanding and not as an end in itself. By preserving a due sense of proportion, the teacher can still keep the lesson oral while avoiding some of the tensions and misconceptions which, as we have seen, may accompany a completely oral presentation lasting several weeks or months. The greatest danger in allowing the student access to the graphic symbol will be that both teacher and student may be tempted to reduce the amount of time devoted to oral repetition. It is this, rather than the use of the written word, which will cause deterioration in oral ability. Here, once again, there will be need for much vigilance on the part of the teacher.

The recent trend toward withholding the written script seems to be traceable to the emphasis of certain schools of linguistic thought, notably the Yale and Prague groups, on the spoken language as the primary substance of linguistic expression. As Moulton says, "The conclusion which they drew . . . was that the student should first be taught to speak the foreign language; teaching him to read it was a totally different and quite separate process—if, indeed, there was time for it at all."[28] Other groups of linguistic scientists, however, of which the Copenhagen school, led by Hjelmslev, may be taken as the leading example, admit the written language on a par with the spoken language and equally worthy of study, drawing attention to the fact that it may be a mere notation of what is spoken.[29] By pleading for the readmission of the graphic symbol to the classroom in the early stages of learning, the writer is referring to a graphic representation of the spoken language and not to literary forms of language far removed from the everyday forms of speech which the audio-lingual method seeks to make automatic in the student's repertoire. Such judicious use of the written script in association with oral practice of the language finds ample support in psychological theory.

---

[28] W. G. Moulton, "Linguistics and Language Teaching in the United States, 1940–1960," in *Trends in European and American Linguistics* (1961), p. 86.

[29] H. Spang-Hanssen, "Glossematics," in *Ibid.*, pp. 147–50.

XI

ASSUMPTION 3
ANALOGY PROVIDES A BETTER FOUNDATION
FOR FOREIGN-LANGUAGE LEARNING
THAN ANALYSIS

THE AUDIO-LINGUAL group does not minimize the importance
of linguistic analysis. They firmly believe that materials for
the study of a foreign language should be prepared by experts with a thorough understanding of the structure of that
language and of the essential differences between it and
the native language of the student. This is, of course, the
conviction of the linguistic scientists.[1] A question arises,
however, of the degree to which analysis of the language
should enter into the learning process.

The general consensus in the sources is that the student
first needs to acquire "a perception of the analogies involved" in the patterns of the language,[2] and to be drilled
in these "until a considerable body of language materials
has been learned."[3] Analysis of the language is regarded
as an advanced study. As Brooks says, "Analogy will guide

---

[1] Fries has stated, "The most efficient materials are those that are
based upon a scientific description of the language to be learned,
carefully compared with a parallel description of the native language
of the learner" (C. C. Fries, *Teaching and Learning English as a
Foreign Language* [Ann Arbor, Mich., 1945], p. 9). Moulton says that
to the linguistic scientists this is the most important emphasis of the
"new method." *Trends in European and American Linguistics, 1930–
1960* (1961), p. 97.

[2] Politzer (1960), p. 15.

[3] *Teacher's Manual* (1961), p. 3.

the learner along the right linguistic path."[4] Brooks considers that analysis may be necessary sometimes for "clearing the track" when a student's prior training has conditioned him to require that he "know what he is doing,"[5] but he warns that this must not be mistaken for advance in the language. Politzer is less convinced that analysis should be completely bypassed at this stage. He cannot see how a "linguistic" approach to teaching can dispense with an explicit or at least an implicit grammatical analysis on the part of the student. The student, he says, must not only learn a construction, he must also realize how this construction is "made up," and how it "comes apart." But, as is consistent with the practice of those who advocate teaching by analogy, he should learn this from what he is observing or doing. In other words, he should be drilled in a structure and, by analogy, in a variety of applications of that structure first. Then, when the structure is thoroughly learned, comes the explanation or "generalization."[6] As Politzer affirms, *"Rules ought to be summaries of behavior. They function only secondarily as 'predictors.'"*[7] Albert Valdman has set out the rationale of this procedure as follows: "In the 'New Key' the function of drill is to induce the subconscious assimilation of the rule; whether the student can or cannot set forth the descriptive statement is of purely academic interest provided he can reproduce the pattern accurately."[8]

In practice, then, the student benefits from the linguistic analysis of experts who have prepared materials which set out the typical patterns of the language, and these the student learns by analogy. Having been drilled in the pattern, "je vais *à l'université*: j'*y* vais," he practices such variants as, "je vais *à l'école*: j'*y* vais" or "il va *à l'église*: il *y* va." When he has practiced this pattern to the point of automatic

---

[4] Brooks (1960), p. 139.

[5] *Ibid.*, p. 47.

[6] Politzer (1961), pp. 5–6.

[7] This is the practice adopted in the units of the Audio-Lingual Materials.

[8] "From Structural Analysis to Pattern Drill," *French Review*, XXXIV, No. 2 (December, 1960), 170.

response, he may be given a generalization which is descriptive of what he has been doing.

Before examining the psychological processes behind analogy and analysis, it is essential to determine the exact meaning of these terms. Webster's New World Dictionary defines "analogy" as "similarity in some respects between things otherwise unlike, partial resemblance," and "analysis" as "a separating or breaking up of any whole into its parts so as to find out their nature, proportion, function, relationship, etc." The issue, then, is whether a foreign language is best learned by memorization and manipulation of patterns which bring out partial resemblances, or similarities of structure, beneath surface variations of vocabulary, or by the study of the component elements of an utterance, their function in the sentence, and their relationship with each other. The former is the basis of "pattern drill," and the latter has been the traditional practice of foreign-language teachers who teach the "grammar" of the language.

To the extent that pattern drill teaches the student a pattern with one group of words and expects him to reproduce it in other similar situations with different vocabulary, it may be considered as basically a process of generalization, in the sense in which psychologists use this term. Teaching a student to examine the component parts of an utterance in order to distinguish their function from that of other parts of the utterance, so that they may be used again in a similar function, may be considered a process of discrimination, in the technical psychological sense.

Generalization is a term used by all behavioristic theorists for the process which occurs when one stimulus, which is to some degree equivalent to another, can substitute for it in arousing a conditioned response. There is a gradient of generalization by which stimuli that are more nearly equivalent to the original stimulus are much more likely to provoke the conditioned response than those which are less similar. Generalization is also dependent on how well the original response has been learned.[9]

There is a major problem to be considered in relation to

---

[9] Hilgard (1956), p. 139; Osgood (1957), p. 351.

generalization (or analogy) as a method of learning a foreign language, namely, what do we take as the criterion of similarity—sound, meaning, function, or form? Meaning is outlawed by some practitioners of pattern drill and is dangerous as a criterion in this case, since the only "meaning" the student knows in the beginning is the native-language meaning, which can lead him to many false assumptions about the patterning of the foreign language. If function is taken as the criterion, then analysis is necessary to determine this function before practice by analogy can take place. Form, as a purely visual pattern without understanding of function, can be very misleading. In any case, with a strictly audio-lingual method it is not available for examination, as the method advocates aural-oral learning of the pattern before visual materials are presented. We are left then with a sound pattern as the basis of similarity. However, this can be a very poor criterion as examination of the following examples, which Politzer has set down for practice by analogy, will show. After *je vais à l'université* and *je vais à l'école*, with *à l'université* and *à l'école* both replaced by *y* (*j'y vais*), he proceeds immediately to use *je parle à mon ami* as an example of a different pattern.[10] How is the student trained by analogy to know that this does not follow the first pattern and become *j'y parle*? If this is considered a *non sequitur* because the *à* expression does not follow *vais*, how is the student to know that *je pense à la leçon* becomes *j'y pense*? Sound in each case is similar in the second part of the pattern, dissimilar in the first part. Politzer goes on to say that "the student who has perceived the fact that *à something* is replaced by the pronoun *y* has understood the grammatical point these sentences are meant to illustrate."[11] If the student has been guided purely by sound, he will not have been able to decide that *à something* was involved and not *à somebody*. If he has made this decision, then he has made a discrimination and analysis has begun to enter in. If he does not make such discriminations, generalization of sound patterns will lead him into many false analogies.

---

10 Politzer (1961), p. 15.
11 *Ibid.*, p. 17.

It would appear, then, with no sure criterion available to the student, that the teacher is the only person in the situation who can decide authoritatively what may be considered similar and so set the limits for generalization. If such false analogies are to be avoided, two courses appear to be open to the teacher: he can either teach the student in drills all the cases in which the pattern is acceptable or else train the student to discriminate in some way between cases which are analogous and those which are not. This the audio-lingual method does in the "generalizations" presented to the class *after* the patterns have been thoroughly learned. From the psychological point of view, this means providing a corrective discrimination after a great deal of generalization has gone on through the pattern drill, rather than training in discrimination at an early stage of the learning process. This facet of the method will be discussed in more detail as the argument develops.

Discrimination is the process by which limits are set to generalization, and individuals are taught to make distinctions between things that are similar but may not be considered equivalent for the purposes of the operation. It is therefore the converse of generalization, where things that are similar are treated as equivalent. By differential reinforcement of responses, an individual can be led to make finer and finer distinctions among what may originally have appeared to be very similar stimuli. Discrimination is then a corrective to maladjustive generalizations.[12] If the structure of a language is taught by careful examination of the functions of words and their relationships,[13] the teacher can train the student to make fine distinctions in grammatical function. This training in discrimination is a long process and involves a certain amount of trial-and-error learning, with the teacher correcting the errors and rewarding the acceptable responses. Finally, however, the student himself is able to act as a critic of the acceptability of his own utterances in the foreign language and becomes in-

---

[12] Miller and Dollard (1941), p. 45.
[13] Hilgard (1956), pp. 442–45, gives a full description of experiments which have demonstrated that discrimination learning may apply to relationships between stimuli as well as to specific stimuli.

dependent to some extent of his teacher.[14] The proponents of the audio-lingual method object to this type of teaching on the ground that the student tends to lose sight of the complete utterance and cannot put the pieces together fast enough for fluent use of the language (or for what they call "automatic response").

An important human characteristic which the method of analogy does not seem to take into account is the individual's desire to understand what he is doing. Both Brooks and Politzer admit the existence of this trait but seem to regard it as rather inconvenient and restrictive. Politzer would counter it by supplying "pseudo-explanations,"[15] and Brooks would defer to an anxious student's desire for explanations in the beginning to ease his mind, but he makes it clear that he considers this attitude a hindrance to the student's advance in the language. "Explanations," he says, "should be circumvented."[16] Both the functionalist and Gestalt theorists, however, have taken seriously this human desire to know what one is doing. Woodworth, for instance, says, "To see, to hear—to see clearly, to hear distinctly—to make out what it is one is seeing or hearing—moment by moment, such concrete immediate motives dominate the life of relation with the environment."[17] Wertheimer goes still further and, consistent with the Gestalt emphasis on man's perception of his environment, states that "to live in a fog . . . is for many people an unbearable state of affairs. There is a tendency to structural clearness, surveyability."[18] Students who are presented with analogical patterns without any explanations of the bases of similarity will tend to establish such bases themselves, if only as a mnemonic device.[19] These superimposed explanations may be quite spurious and may lead to generalization in quite wrong directions. Students of low intelligence are, of course, much

---

[14] Compare the description of discrimination training in the teaching of singing in Miller and Dollard (1941), pp. 153–59.

[15] Politzer (1960), p. 17.

[16] Brooks (1960), pp. 47, 124.

[17] R. Woodworth, "Reinforcement of Perception" (1947), quoted in Hilgard (1956), p. 467.

[18] Wertheimer (1945), p. 199.

[19] Miller, Galanter, and Pribram (1960) discuss at some length (chap. x) the ways people organize material they have to remember.

happier just repeating what is given to them, and do not feel a strong compulsion to understand what they are doing,[20] but this same low intelligence also makes it hard for them to see analogies. The very fact that the Miller Analogy Test is used as a screening test for students wishing to undertake advanced studies is an indication that the perception of analogies is not considered the commonest of intellectual capacities.[21]

An examination of Gestalt conclusions may be useful in this area, especially as our students have been left dependent upon perception of sound patterns. Although this research was not based on foreign-language learning, the conclusions apply to the process of learning in general, and seem appropriate to this analogy-analysis discussion.

The audio-lingual approach appears at first sight to be consistent with Gestalt psychology. It is a revolt against a piecemeal grammatical approach, in which the language is taken apart, the parts are studied separately, and the student is expected to put them together again in a form as closely related to the original as possible. In contrast to this procedure, the audio-lingual method of learning by analogy through pattern drill proposes to present complete structures to the student to be learned as "wholes," and language-learning becomes, as Politzer says, "the perception of a 'gestalt,' an awareness of a pattern or configuration of patterns."[22]

---

[20] In the *Study of the Effectiveness of Language Laboratories*, conducted by Raymond Keating for the Institute of Administrative Research at Teachers College, Columbia University, it was found that the students of low and average intelligence seemed to gain as much from language laboratory drill as from classroom teaching, whereas, in most skill areas, especially after the first year, those of superior intelligence did not (R. Keating [1963], p. 28).

[21] Politzer says, "The ability to see such relations is essentially a function of 'scholastic aptitude' or 'Intelligence' as measured in most of the conventional I.Q. or scholastic or verbal aptitude examinations. It seems thus inevitable that we should find a rather high correlation between a student's general intelligence and his ability to control the pattern mechanism of a foreign language" (p. 15). See also Pimsleur, Mosberg, and Morrison, "Student Factors in Foreign Language Learning: A Review of the Literature" (1960), in Pimsleur (1961), for a discussion of the experiments and studies of the relationship between intelligence and foreign-language achievement (p. 1).

[22] Politzer (1960), p. 15.

Politzer's statement, however, is an oversimplification of the Gestalt position. It is true that Wertheimer, for instance, urges us to keep the whole in view, and let the whole dominate the parts, but a closer examination of what he says shows a constant emphasis on understanding the structure of the whole. The perception of a "gestalt" involves an understanding of "the harmony in the mutual requirements" within the structure.[23] When ready-made solutions are provided (and this is the case with pattern drills), Wertheimer says, "For real understanding one has to re-create the steps, the structural inner relatedness, the requiredness."[24] This involves analysis. The student must realize that a language is not just what Wertheimer calls an "and-summation" of patterns, but that these patterns are structurally related to the whole language design, and that within them there are separate, functioning parts. It is only by acquiring such an understanding of the true "gestalt" of the language that a student can rise above mere facility in manipulating patterns to a genuine *Sprachgefühl* and a command of the language in all its flexibility.

The same understanding of relationships is also important if what is learned is to be retained. Brooks says that a person who has learned how a language works has learned something he will have to forget if he wishes to advance in the use of the language.[25] It is to be hoped that by this statement Brooks does not mean that every pattern in the language will have to be learned individually as though it had no relation to the whole. In the case of a language, the number of patterns to be learned is so inordinately large that it will be impossible to give each one the "saturation practice" which Brooks considers necessary for it to become habitual. As a result, any sections of this enormous load which are not practiced for some time will be subject to fairly rapid extinction. Experiments with rote-learning have shown that some form of grouping and noting of relationships effectively reduces the amount to be learned and retained. As George Miller has stated, "Since

---

23 Wertheimer (1945), p. 195.
24 *Ibid.*, p. 194.
25 Brooks (1960), p. 47.

it is as easy to remember a lot of information (when the items are informationally rich) as it is to remember a little information (when the items are informationally impoverished), it is economical to organize the material into rich chunks . . . . The process of organizing and re-organizing is a pervasive human trait, and it is motivated, at least in part, by an attempt to make the best possible use of our mnemonic capacity."[26] As has already been shown in the discussion on the two levels of language learning, memory is distinctly aided by the understanding of a principle.

Recent research has also demonstrated a positive cor-relation between meaningfulness and the amount of ma-terial learned in a constant time.[27] For the purpose of these experiments, meaningful materials were defined as those which arouse associations from previous experiences. Meaningfulness is thus a matter of learned associations which have a bearing on the material being memorized. As applied to pattern drill, meaningfulness does not imply that the student should be able to give native-language "meanings" for the patterns being studied; such substitu-tion could cause interference from the learned patterns of the native language. It does mean that he must under-stand the composition of the pattern to the extent that he can see the function of the words in relation to each other, this function depending on form, arrangement, and dis-tribution. This is what the linguistic scientists call "structural meaning."[28] Each successive pattern increases in meaningfulness as the understanding of previous pat-terns is brought to bear on it. If the student realizes what kinds of structural transformations he is manipulating, he will be able to make clearer discriminations between the usages of his native language and those of the foreign language. In this way, some of the interference of the native language will be obviated, an interference which is

---

26 G. Miller, "Human Memory and the Storage of Information" (1956) ; quoted in Miller, Galanter, and Pribram (1960), p. 132.

27 McGeoch and Irion (1952), pp. 470–80; and Underwood and Schulz, *Meaningfulness and Verbal Learning* (Chicago, 1960).

28 Fries (1954), in Allen (1958), p. 111. See also chap. xii in this book.

inevitable if contrasts between the foreign language and the native language are not the object of discrimination training.

As McGeoch and Irion have pointed out, "Learning is not a passive chaining of adjacent items, but requires instead, an active analytic mode of response."[29] Blind, repetitive drilling in contrasts, by students who do not perceive them as contrasts, will have much less effect for more effort than the same material drilled by students who understand the relationships within the structure, and who are therefore being drilled in these rather than in simple sound patterns. Whether the terminology used to help the student gain this understanding is the traditional one, that of the linguistic scientists, or some useful terminology invented by the teacher to suit the student's level of maturity, the small amount of time spent by the teacher in explaining the concepts behind the terminology will be amply repaid later, when teacher and class are able to use it as a tool to facilitate explanation and elucidation.

A short explanation of what is being practiced will then result in the student's focusing on those elements in the pattern which he most needs to learn, instead of casting around in his mind for some mnemonic device of rhythm or grouping which will help him remember the sound pattern. This accords well with the Gestalt principles of familiarity and set. If the student is actively looking for some element in the pattern, he is more likely to find it and remember it than if he is not alert to it.[30]

From meaningfulness in the sense of learned associations it is but a step to "meaning" as this term is used in mediation theory. As this theoretical position will be discussed at some length in chapter xii in connection with the fourth assumption, it will be alluded to briefly here. Experiments by Razran and others have shown that considerably more generalization occurs on the basis of similarity of meaning than on the basis of similarity of sound.[31] If, in word association experiments, there is more

---

[29] McGeoch and Irion (1952), p. 479.
[30] Woodworth (1948), p. 130.
[31] These experiments are listed in Mowrer (1960a), pp. 56–57.

generalization of reaction from "joy" to "happiness" than from "joy" to "toy," then some process other than a physical stimulus is operative. Osgood, Mowrer, and others describe the process as a mediating response and stimulus. A mediating response or "meaning" has been established for the experience of joy (happiness, elation), through past associations, and it is this mediating response which acts as a stimulus for behavior resulting from the hearing of the word "joy." Hence the familiar S-R (stimulus-response) formula is replaced by S-r_m-s_m-R (stimulus-mediating response-mediating stimulus-response). In the case of the joy-happiness and joy-toy associations, then, the word "happiness" arouses a mediating reaction similar to that aroused by the word "joy"[32] so that generalization occurs, whereas the similarity of sound of "joy" and "toy" is inconsequential and generalization is therefore much less likely to occur. Since analogy is a form of generalization, this theory lends support to the notion that meaningfulness will make for better learning by analogy as well as for better learning by analysis.

The ultimate aim of either of these methods of learning is transfer of what has been learned in a particular situation, with specific utterances, to other situations. If the student is unable to do this, he will never be able to use the language for his own purposes. Transfer must not be assumed to be automatic, any more than we can presume that a child "learns" because he is taught. In other words, because students are taught how to manipulate linguistic structures and responses in a directed situation we cannot assume that this will automatically give them facility in using the language in undirected situations. Research in the area of transfer has called attention to certain factors which affect this process, and these must be understood if the student is to get the maximum benefit from his classroom study of the foreign language.

First of all, it is important to keep in mind that "after small amounts of learning early in the life of the individual, every instance of learning is a function of the already

---

[32] See Osgood (1953), p. 402, for an explanation of this phenomenon.

existent learned organization of the subject; that is, all learning is influenced by transfer."[33] Much as we might like to exclude from the learning of the foreign language all influence of native-language learning, this is impossible. By accepting the inevitable, we can use the elements of native-language learning which will help foreign-language learning, such as learned ability to imitate sounds, understanding of functions of words, elements of patterning which are for practical purposes identical in the two languages, existing concepts which are similar to the new concepts, and reading skill, thus reducing to some degree the time necessary for learning the new language.

At the same time, steps must be taken to guard against negative transfer, or interference from the native language, where learned elements associated with it are incompatible with elements of the new language. Warning about these danger points through the teaching of contrasts between the native language and the foreign language, as advocated by the linguistic scientists, can help the student to avoid such pitfalls. This is consistent with Osgood's mediation theory. Where there is great similarity between a native language word, pattern, or tense but a different meaning or application in the foreign language (this includes what French teachers have long called "faux amis"), the foreign-language stimulus tends to arouse the native-language meaning reaction and so cause negative transfer. By directly teaching the difference, the teacher is establishing a separate meaning reaction for the new foreign-language term or structure, and in the future the probability of this new meaning's being aroused, instead of the original native-language meaning, will increase as this reaction is strengthened through practice. If the difference between them is not expressly taught, the teacher may not have occasion to discover that the distinction has never occurred to the student, who may have accepted the negative transfer as positive transfer.

There are two major positions in psychological theory with regard to positive transfer—that originating with

---

[33] McGeoch and Irion (1952), p. 346.

Thorndike and emphasizing the transfer of identical elements, and the Gestalt version, called transposition.[34] According to Thorndike, transfer occurs when specific elements which have been learned reappear in a new situation. These elements need not be facts; they may also be elements of method or attitude. Elements of patterns practiced in pattern drill will transfer to situations where the stimulus words or phrases are the same, and ability to manipulate parts of a sentence will transfer to a new situation where this skill is appropriate. Thus, in the case of simple everyday phrases where the stimuli are comparatively unvarying, experience in class with patterns and memorized dialogues will transfer to the new situation. Such experience does not, however, train the student in selecting from available responses the ones which are appropriate to novel stimuli, or in rearranging elements of learned responses to fit new occasions. Thorndike's view is consistent with the method of teaching language by analogy, and is well suited to the manipulative level of foreign-language learning.

According to the Gestalt view of transposition, what transfers to a new situation is perceived relationships. Common principles mediate learning between two situations which are otherwise quite different. These provide much better transfer than reliance on similar elements which, in the crucial situation, may not reappear or may not be perceived as reappearing.[35] This view, it will be remembered,[36] is the one behind Katona's learning with understanding which was found to be appropriate to the selective level of language learning. Its relationship to analysis of the principles at work in foreign-language structure is evident.

Other areas in which transfer occurs, according to ex-

---

[34] A useful discussion of the subject of transfer will be found in Blair, Jones, and Simpson (1962), pp. 289–94.

[35] This is known as Humphrey's Arpeggio Paradox. The nature of the reaction depends upon the context. Subjects may be trained by shock conditioning to raise their hands on hearing a particular musical tone and yet not respond at all when they hear it as part of a well-known tune. See Osgood (1956), p. 210.

[36] See chap. vi.

perimental research, are those of set and attitudes. The way a student perceives a new situation is the result of transfer from previous similar situations. If his work in the foreign-language class has caused him to perceive the manipulation of linguistic structures and the repetition of foreign-language phrases as "class exercises," unrelated to real-life concerns, then these are not likely to spring readily to his mind in a real-life situation, and he will tend to resort to his own language for actual communication, even with foreigners. If, however, in his work in class, he has been taught to perceive the foreign language as a tool for expressing his thoughts and for communicating with others, then this will help him to break through the initial barrier of shyness which most individuals have to face when they have the first opportunity to use their classroom-acquired knowledge of a foreign language in an actual encounter with native speakers of that language.

The transfer of attitudes has already been discussed at some length in the section on conditioning and is satisfactorily explained by Mowrer's theory of emotional conditioning. In cases where foreign-language study in school has involved unpleasant and embarrassing experiences, foreign-language responses can arouse stimuli which have been conditioned to emotions of anxiety and disappointment, and will therefore be associated with attitudes of avoidance. On the other hand, where the classroom study of the language has been pleasant and interesting, foreign-language words or phrases will arouse stimuli associated with pleasant emotions of expectancy. In this way, attitudes developed in the classroom will transfer to the real-life foreign-language situation.

One point which stands out very clearly from the research on transfer is that, in order for transfer from classroom to real-life situations to be really effective, the classroom practice must simulate the requirements of an actual language interchange as closely as possible. An abstracted, academic study of a foreign language, as many unfortunate students will testify, does not lead to transfer. We learn what we practice, as Guthrie has said.[37] If the

---

[37] Hilgard (1948), p. 64.

student practices abstracting examples of the peculiarities of a foreign language from the matrix of speech and writing, examining them in the light of grammatical rules and endeavoring to generate similar ones which follow these rules, this is what he will learn. If he practices giving correct responses in drill sessions so as to get good grades, he will become very adept at this. If he is taught to understand the structure of a language, so that he may be able to practice using it correctly as a tool of communication, this is what he will learn. It is obvious then that, if the most effective transfer to a foreign-language communication situation is to take place, every opportunity must be provided for the students to use the language for communication in the classroom.

Our discussion of the virtues and shortcomings of analogy and analysis brings out the fact that they serve different purposes. Each is a valuable learning procedure in itself, but they are appropriate to different levels of language behavior. If language behavior is hierarchical, as has been suggested, then analysis and the understanding of structure are essential for the over-all direction of communication, whereas analogy is a useful procedure for automatizing the details of language structure at the manipulative level.

In *Words and Things*, Roger Brown gives as his considered opinion that "the intellectual essence of language behavior is not a matter of the number of utterances to which appropriate reactions can be trained nor even of the complication of these utterances. From experiences of particular utterances and their referents a child learns to produce new responses which have not been specifically practiced but which conform to the rules of the language. He interiorizes a system for generating appropriate behavior rather than a list of rote responses."[38] The child learns language largely by analogy, making many mistakes as he goes along and taking a long time to perfect his utterances. The high-school student is considerably older and therefore capable of many more logical processes than

---

[38] Roger Brown, *Words and Things* (Glencoe, Ill., 1958), p. 182.

the child.[39] It is possible for him to take short-cuts by analysis, so that he can learn in 700 to 800 class-hours what the child has taken years to learn. By developing understanding of structure through analysis and by practicing manipulation of linguistic structures by analogy, he can achieve mastery of a foreign language both at the level of formation of correct phrases and in the more demanding area of organizing the expression of complex ideas. Whether his analysis is performed from the point of view of traditional or transformational grammar, it is essential for him to have an understanding of the underlying structure of the sentence in order to be able to bring about the innumerable changes and permutations which fluent use of the language requires.

Hence we see the value of what Miller, Galanter, and Pribram have called "metaplans"—formulas, sets of rules, generalizations. These are "Plans to generate Plans" of grammatical usage, and when the appropriate moment comes "they can be projected into an infinite variety of unforeseen situations."[40] These are the master Plans that enable the individual to face up to any conversational situation, but for real fluency the student will need to have had considerable practice in putting Plans of the subordinate type into rapid operation, through some such procedure as pattern drill.

---

[39] B. Inhelder and J. Piaget, *The Growth of Logical Thinking from Childhood to Adolescence* (New York, 1958).

[40] Miller, Galanter, and Pribram (1960), p. 178.

XII

ASSUMPTION 4

THE MEANING WHICH THE WORDS OF A
LANGUAGE HAVE FOR THE NATIVE SPEAKER
CAN BE LEARNED ONLY IN A MATRIX OF
ALLUSIONS TO THE CULTURE OF THE
PEOPLE WHO SPEAK THAT LANGUAGE[1]

"MEANING" as a concept has proved to be difficult for both
the linguistic scientist and the psychologist to examine.
Both were wary of approaching it by introspection. To the
older school of behaviorists, the notion of meaning as it
is generally understood is mentalistic, empirically un-
demonstrable, and unnecessary for an explanation of
behavior. Linguistic scientists rejected the idea of a
meaning absolute in any language, which could be found
in a dictionary, and stated that dictionary meanings were
synonyms or paraphrases which left the question, "What
is the meaning?" unanswered. "The so-called lexical meanings in certain signs are nothing but artificially isolated
contextual meanings, or artificial paraphrases of them,"
says Hjelmslev. "In absolute isolation no sign has any
meaning."[2]

In examining language structure, many linguistic
scientists prefer to disregard what Fries has called "social-

---

[1] "Culture" is used here in the sociological and anthropological sense.
As Politzer (1961) expresses it, "Culture . . . is the entire complex
pattern of behavior and material achievements which are produced,
learned, and shared by the members of a community" (p. 130).

[2] L. Hjelmslev, *Prolegomena to a Theory of Language* (Madison,
Wis., 1961).

cultural meaning"[3] and to concentrate on contextual and structural meaning. They study the distribution of a linguistic item in a corpus of utterances and identify "meaning" as a function of the sets in which the item occurs and of its relationships with other elements in the contrastive patterns of the language. Joos has stated categorically, "Let the sociologists keep the outside or practical meaning; then we can undertake to describe the pure linguistic meaning. . . . The linguist's meaning of a morpheme is by definition the set of conditional probabilities of its occurrence in context with all other morphemes."[4]

It is this approach to language which has led some experimenters in the field of foreign-language teaching to propose a period of training in a new language without any explanation of traditionally defined meaning, concentrating on structural and contextual meaning.[5] What has proved a useful approach in language analysis and description cannot, however, be automatically transferred to the area of foreign-language teaching, where relationships between individuals are involved, without serious consideration of psychological factors. Most foreign-language teachers will agree with Fries, who is not only an eminent linguistic scientist but has also been for many years a leader in methods of teaching English as a foreign language, when he says that "linguistic meaning without social-cultural meaning constitutes . . . 'mere verbalism.' "[6]

The Swiss linguistic scientist, De Saussure, has drawn a useful distinction in the area of language between "langue" and "parole." "Langue" is the social convention of language which the child learns as an apprentice. It "is not complete in any speaker; it exists perfectly only within a collectivity." "Parole," on the other hand, is the individual, executive side of speech, "the combinations by which the speaker uses the language code for expressing his own thought."[7] It is "langue" that we teach, in order that the

---

[3] Fries (1954), in Allen (1958), p. 112.

[4] M. Joos, "Description of Language Design," in *Readings in Linguistics* (New York, 1958), p. 356.

[5] Oinas (1960), pp. 121–42.

[6] Fries (1954), in Allen (1958), p. 112.

[7] Saussure (1959), p. 14.

student may be able to use "parole" in communication with native speakers of the language. It is "langue" that we set out in our textbooks, on our tapes, and on the sound-tracks of our films—the average which has been set up by many individuals using the same sign system. This average has evolved from the experiences of many persons in the social situation. Thus "every language is a model of a culture and of its adjustment to the world."[8] If our students are to be able to use the foreign language to express their personal meaning in a way which will be comprehensible to a native speaker, they must move beyond linguistic or distributional meaning into this area of social convention in use of words, tone of voice, and intonation.

The social and cultural aspect of meaning was one of the great interests of Edward Sapir, who was a lifelong student of language. To him, language was "a perfect symbolism of experience,"[9] and "the understanding of a simple poem" involved "not merely an understanding of the single words in their average significance, but a full comprehension of the whole life of the community as it is mirrored in the words, or as it is suggested by their overtones."[10] To Sapir, our whole view of the world is shaped by the language we learned as a child. "The 'real world,'" he says, "is to a large extent unconsciously built up on the language habits of the group. No two languages are ever sufficiently similar to be considered as representing the same social reality. The worlds in which different societies live are distinct worlds, not merely the same world with different labels attached."[11] This thesis has been further developed by Whorf, who tried to show from his study of the language of the Hopi Indians how their world-view was closely related to the grammatical categories of their language.[12] Although his hypothesis is

---

[8] Hill (1958), p. 9.

[9] D. Mandelbaum (ed.), *Selected Writings of Edward Sapir* (Berkeley, Calif., 1958), p. 12.

[10] *Ibid.*, p. 162.

[11] *Ibid.*

[12] The Whorfian hypothesis is discussed at length in *Language in Culture*, ed. H. Hoijer (Chicago, 1954).

not considered proved, it has had a great influence on thinking in the area of "social-cultural meaning."

Even if we do not fully accept the Sapir-Whorfian hypothesis that our ways of looking at the world are derived from the categories of our language, experience with other languages soon reveals significant differences in the areas which are included in these categories. Hjelmslev, who was very impressed by Sapir's work, expressed this idea in a delightful way: "Each language," he said, "lays down its own boundaries within the amorphous 'thought-mass' and stresses different factors in it in different arrangements, puts the centers of gravity in different places and gives them different emphases. It is like one and the same handful of sand that is formed in quite different patterns, or like the cloud in the heavens that changes shape in Hamlet's view from minute to minute."[13] These categories are learned by the child as he actively shares in the life of the community around him. In order to speak a foreign language effectively, the student must learn to use categories in the same way as the native speaker if he is to avoid false impressions and frequent misunderstandings.

Just as in linguistic science there are scholars who seek to penetrate the thought-processes indicated by differences in language categories, so in psychology there is a movement to examine what takes place between stimulus and verbal response in a human reaction. As experimentation in the area of verbal behavior has developed, an increasing number of psychologists have felt that some intervening process must be postulated if the results are to be explained. Mediation theorists have been particularly interested in research in this area. Osgood and his colleagues, for instance, devote a great deal of time and thought to analyzing and measuring the components of "meaning" by statistical procedures. In this way, they try to establish a "semantic space within which the meaning of any concept can be specified."[14] This semantic space is multidimensional, taking meaning beyond the stage of mere reference to particular objects, events, or categories. It is interesting to note

[13] Hjelmslev (1961), p. 52.
[14] Osgood, Suci, and Tannenbaum (1957), p. 38.

that the semantic differential, as the measuring instrument
is called, has already brought out national differences in
the "meaning" of certain terms, as linguistic theories had
foreseen.

The work of Osgood and his associates in the factor
analysis of meaning has shown that it contains a considerable evaluative element. In *The Measurement of Meaning*,
the writers state that their results "suggest that the
evaluative factor plays a dominant role in meaningful
judgments."[15] A large part of the total variance is still
unaccounted for, however, including, presumably, the
cognitive element. Mowrer refers to these two elements as
"images of value" and "images of fact," using "image"
in the sense of conditioned sensation,[16] and these provide
an interesting parallel to what are commonly called the
connotative and denotative aspects of meaning.

What Osgood intends by his use of the term "meaning"
is made clear in his mediation theory. Here his crucial
concept is that of a "sign." "A pattern of stimulation which
is not the object is a sign of the object if it evokes in an
organism a mediating reaction, this (a) being some fractional part of the total behavior elicited by the object
and (b) producing distinctive self-stimulation that mediates
responses which would not occur without the previous association of nonobject and object patterns of stimulation."[17]

Diagrammatically, the mediation hypothesis as applied
to verbal behavior would appear as follows:

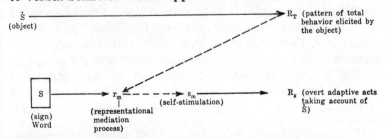

Words as signs, Osgood says, "become conditioned to some
distinctive portion of the total object reaction, this portion

---

15 *Ibid.*, p. 38.
16 Mowrer (1960*b*), p. 165.
17 Osgood (1953), p. 696.

coming to function in behavior as a representational mediation process (r_m). This process is representational because it is part of the very same behavior that the thing signified produces, hence its symbolic, semantic property; it is a mediation process by virtue of the fact that the self-stimulation it produces (s_m) can become associated with a variety of overt adaptive acts (R_x) which 'take account of' the thing signified."[18] r_m represents psychological meaning, and linguistic responses are a subset of R_x.

The connotative meaning of a word contains a large element of emotion, e.g. anxiety, whereas the denotative meaning refers particularly to visual, tactual, or proprioceptive effects. As Sapir has said, "It is because it is learned early and piecemeal, in constant association with the color and the requirements of actual contexts, that language, in spite of its quasi-mathematical form, is rarely a purely referential organization."[19]

If Osgood's theory of meaning is accepted, then it is obvious that the meaning of any word in a foreign language is closely related to behavior in the foreign culture toward the object or process for which it stands and the experiences of a native-born member of the culture in relation to that object.[20] Take, for example, the word "escargot," which to a Frenchman "means" the satisfactions of a special dinner, perhaps the associated pleasures of dining out, or, to a Burgundian, sensations of "home." Translated as "snail," it "means" to an American a slimy creature to be avoided, to be crushed or poisoned in order to protect the vegetable garden. If "concierge" means "janitor," then half the humorous allusions in French speech to this ubiquitous character lose their piquancy.

Koffka says, in Gestalt terms, that we live and move each in his "behavioral environment" which is organized according to our own experience of the real environment,

---

[18] C. Osgood, "Studies on the Generality of Affective Meaning Systems," *American Psychologist*, XVII (January, 1962). See also Osgood (1953), pp. 695–99. There is an interesting discussion of Osgood's theory of "meaning" in Lambert (1963), Part I, pp. 52–53.

[19] Mandelbaum (1958), p. 12.

[20] "Object" is being used here in the sense of physical object, event, or concept.

and this is relevant to Osgood's formulation, which is an attempt to find a common meeting ground for stimulus-response behaviorist psychology and Gestalt psychology. Our own experience is, however, profoundly influenced by the culture into which we have been born. As G. Miller has said, "The intimate relation of verbal habits to the way we perceive the world about us is a familiar fact to psychologists. Many of the differences we perceive among things and events would not be noticed if society had not forced us to learn that they have different names."[21] This is what Roger Brown has called "cognitive socialization . . . ; learning to structure experience and thought as they are structured by the social group,"[22] and many studies have been made of language differences as they reflect cultural attitudes and experiences.[23] In his book, *The Silent Language,* in which he attempts to lay methodological foundations for a theory of culture, Edward Hall says, "We must never assume that we are fully aware of what we communicate to someone else. There exists in the world today tremendous distortions in meaning as men try to communicate with one another. The job of achieving understanding and insight into mental processes of others is much more difficult and the situation more serious than most of us care to admit."[24]

The work of the foreign-language teacher is to help the student to penetrate beyond certain muscular movements and organized sound impressions to the experiences which these physical phenomena represent to the native speaker. Some teachers will protest that this is not their task, that they have only to teach the student the language in its accepted spoken and written form, so that he can use it to communicate with other people who use that language and to read what they have written. The words themselves contain their own meaning. This fits well with what Malinowski has called the "bucket theory of

---

[21] G. Miller (1951), p. 199.

[22] R. Brown (1958), p. 19.

[23] Eugene Nida's book, *"God's Word in Man's Language"* (New York, 1952), is a rich source of anecdotes which illustrate this fact.

[24] E. T. Hall, *The Silent Language* (New York, 1959), p. 52.

meaning"—that "words like little buckets are assumed to pick up their loads of meaning in one mind, carry them across intervening space, and dump them in another mind."[25] If, however, we accept Mowrer's view that "in communication . . . we are transferring meanings *from sign to sign* within a given person," then this person "must already *have* the meanings with which we shall be dealing;"[26] we are merely arousing these particular meanings and associating them in new ways. It becomes of paramount importance, then, that we should be aware of the "meanings" we are arousing when we use a foreign tongue. This is problem enough in our own language, where lack of comprehension of what seem to us to be familiar expressions often clears with the words, "So *that's* what you meant!"

In his endeavor to guide his students into the "meanings" words have for the native speaker, the foreign-language teacher will need to keep in mind the four behavioral relations of signs which can be derived from Osgood's formulation. Osgood has called these the representing relation, the mediating relation, the empathic relation, and the communicating relation.[27]

The representing relation is the one that exists between signs and their referents. This refers to the categories in which the native speaker places things. In a Western European language, for instance, French, it may seem to us at a superficial level that these categories are the same as our own. To take a gross example, we may identify the French meaning of "champignon" with the English or American meaning of "mushroom." A glance at the page in *Le Petit Larousse* illustrating "Champignons" will soon reveal the lack of correspondence. Or we may note the different sensory categorization implied by "parfum" and "perfume." The "parfum" of ice cream would certainly never fit into the English category.

The mediating relation is that between the self-stimu-

---

[25] B. Malinowski, "The Problem of Learning in Primitive Languages" (Supplement in Ogden and Richards, *The Meaning of Meaning* [1938]; quoted in Osgood [1953], p. 680.

[26] Mowrer (1960*b*), p. 139.

[27] Osgood (1953), p. 698.

lation and the overt response, a relation composed of hierarchies of habits, their relative strengths depending on "momentary contextual conditions and pervasive cultural factors." At the sound of his own voice saying "Bonjour, monsieur," the Frenchman automatically extends his hand.

The empathic relation refers to the relation between the response made to a sign and that made to the object represented. This may vary from an identical response to a very different one. In certain contexts, the word "apple" may arouse the same mouth-watering reactions as the sight of the fruit itself. On the other hand, a Frenchman may have feelings of complete indifference to camels, yet react violently if someone says to him, "Chameau!"

The communicating relation is the relation between mediation processes and particular classes of instrumental skill sequences (such as linguistic skills). This particular relation finds its expression in the acceptable structures and vocabulary of the language, which the foreigner must learn to manipulate in the same way as the native speaker if he is to convey the "meaning" he intends. The problems involved in developing these language habits in students have already been discussed in earlier chapters.

The foreign-language teacher must be conscious of the existence of these four relations if he is to do justice to "meaning" in the foreign language as well as to manipulative skill. Such a consciousness can come only through long study of the language and contact with speakers of that language, or, if this is impossible, extensive reading of all kinds of material in the foreign language (literature, magazines, newspapers) which show how people of that culture think and react currently. Ideally, the foreign language should be learned in as close association as practicable with the culture of the country where it is spoken, if its full "meaning" is to be plumbed to any depth. As Hockett has said, "The shortcut of asking what a form means must ultimately be supplemented by active participation in the life of the community."[28] This will not be possible for most students, but the alert teacher will attempt to make up

---

[28] C. Hockett, *A Course in Modern Linguistics* (New York, 1958), p. 141.

this deficiency by using every possible device to bring his students into close contact with the culture through the use of "realia" from the country concerned: films, songs, visits from native speakers, introduction to the history, geography, customs, art, music, and the works of the molders of thought and attitudes of the country where the language is spoken. As the Modern Language Association's foreign language policy statement says: "The study of a foreign language . . . is both a progressive *experience* and a progressive acquisition of a skill."[29]

A major factor militating against the achievement of these objectives is that of motivation. Wallace Lambert and his colleagues have recently conducted a number of experiments on the *Roles of Attitudes and Motivation in Second Language Learning*. These studies show that "the student who has ethnocentric or prejudiced attitudes toward foreign peoples and who makes invidious comparisons of French with American ways of life is likely to do poorly in school French and in some aspects of comprehension, independent of any intellectual capacity or motivation to do well in French."[30] A further study shows that "American students of English-speaking backgrounds who are in the process of studying the French language have a generally negative set of stereotypes about the basic personality characteristics of French-speaking people."[31] The finding that this is a major handicap to the development of a "progressive experience" through the learning of French is supported by studies on set and attitude. Prejudices of this type against French-speaking people impart a negative valence to learning their language. As Lewin has shown, this negative valence inheres not in the object itself but in the object as perceived by the person, and can be changed only by a change in meaning of the goal-related activity.[32] Curran's study at Loyola University, Chicago, showed that each student selected for

[29] In "Values of Foreign Language Study," *PMLA* (September, 1956), Part II.
[30] Lambert (1961), p. 36.
[31] *Ibid.*, p. 132.
[32] Hilgard (1956), pp. 266, 279.

the experiment seemed to have "to a surprising degree
personal and sometimes even traumatic emotional blocking"
against one or more of the four languages chosen for the
experiment, "going back sometimes to early childhood."[33]
It is essential that material which is used to give a
deeper understanding of the culture of another people
should be very carefully prepared so as not to confirm the
American student's stereotype of the people. Lambert's
experiments showed that American students regarded the
Frenchman, for instance, as being "less thoughtful, less
intelligent, clearly less honest and dependable, less generous, less kind, less reliable, less stable, and having less
character" than an English-speaking person, as well as
being "more humorous and entertaining, very likely in the
sense that he is somewhat ridiculous."[34] Any experienced
teacher of French can immediately call to mind a number
of examples of reading material, commonly provided in
school textbooks, which would support many characteristics
of this stereotype. Such unfavorable impressions are
particularly likely to develop when the student is presented
with a diet of reading material and surrounded by realia
depicting the customs and attitudes of the foreign people
in a different century, or in a radically different social
milieu from that of the student himself. Unless it is made
clear to the student that this picture of the foreign people
is of historical, antiquarian, or sociological interest, he may
accept the situations, customs, and ways of thinking described as being typical of contemporary life in the foreign
society. This will inevitably lead him to look upon these
foreign people, so obviously ill-adapted to the modern
world, as ridiculous, or, at the very least, peculiar and
quaint.

It is possible that some foreign-language teachers, whose
own acquaintance with the foreign culture is superficial
and who themselves have never shared in the experience
of the real "meaning" of the language (as Osgood uses the
term), also subscribe to the sort of stereotype described

---

[33] Curran (1961), p. 89. A detailed description of this experiment
is given in chap. ix, Part II, in this book.
[34] Lambert (1961), p. 132.

by Lambert and then wonder why they cannot increase their students' motivation to learn the language. A matrix of allusions to another culture cannot help the student to comprehend the real "meaning" of the language unless their selection and presentation are most carefully analyzed in the light of "meanings" which will be imposed by American students. Although Lambert's findings related specifically to the study of French, teachers of other modern foreign languages will immediately recognize parallels with their own situation. Often a short explanation of a cultural situation, as proposed by some proponents of the audio-lingual method, is essential to bring about associations of meanings within the mind of the student which will approximate the "meaning" the situation has for a native speaker. The words and patterns learned with such associations in mind will thus be more likely to be appropriately used or fully understood, and in this way will lead to actual communication with native speakers instead of misunderstanding and misinterpretation.

This approach to meaning highlights one of the dangers of the Direct Method, which tries to arouse meanings in the mind of the student by direct association of foreign word with object or situation. With a pure Direct Method, it is difficult to keep a check on the accuracy of the meanings being aroused, and many incorrect assumptions based on the student's own culture may well be reinforced without the teacher's knowledge.[35]

In our native culture, meanings are reinforced by repetition in a great variety of contexts and situations. The dialogue method, with its "real-life" situations, attempts to meet this need, especially when expressions are used in a number of dialogues with varying applications and are then used freely in the classroom situation. There is not, however, sufficient time during a student's school career, with a limited number of foreign-language lessons

---

[35] Hebb (1949), p. 132, and McGeoch and Irion (1952), p. 479, both bring out the fact, demonstrated in experiments with nonsense syllables and rote learning, that where no meaningful relations are apparent, the subjects will invent their own. This may happen with the Direct Method.

each week, for him to adapt and reassociate all the shades of meanings from a multiplicity of contexts. For this reason, the audio-lingual method of supplying an idiomatic native-language version in the early stages of the learning of a dialogue, without emphasis or undue study, would appear to be sound. In this way, distinctions and differences can be brought out clearly and promptly; the student can then be directed back to the foreign-language version with fewer misconceptions, and the learning of the new meanings can be reinforced by practice and use. Trial-and-error approximations to meaning on the part of the student will be avoided, and more will be accomplished in the time available.

One thing which is sacrificed in this approach is vividness of presentation of new expressions. Where the student is beginning the language early, and has six or seven years of study ahead of him, his interest may be caught and held by the problem element in a direct presentation of concrete concepts by visual means, as an adaptation of the discovery method. This vividness of presentation arouses an attention set on his part which will aid learning and retention. The difficulties of misconceptions are less likely to occur at this early age, because the material chosen as suitable to the interests of younger children will deal much more with concrete objects and everyday experiences which are easy to present visually.[36] Some modern textbooks are accompanied by film strips and films which contain sufficient authentic situational material to minimize the possibility of the formation of inexact concepts and thus make more feasible the direct association of foreign word and concept.

A great deal of foreign-language knowledge is acquired through context. This is the way we continue to increase our knowledge of our own language. Osgood points to four

---

[36] Even in this situation, it is doubtful whether the students make a "direct" association. The experiments of Karwoski, Gramlich, and Arnott (1944), described in Osgood (1953), p. 711, suggest that "both object and pictorial stimuli required an intermediary symbol before a verbal response to them could be made. It is also probable that for both object and pictorial presentations the dominant tendency to label them interfered with other possible verbal responses."

types of context, and each of these is important for foreign-language teachers.[37]

First, there is the internal nonverbal context, composed of emotional and motivational states, which influences the choice of words as well as the tone of voice. This can be conveyed by the teacher in the teaching of dialogues by mimicry, or by tape recordings of the dialogues if the teacher himself has not a sufficiently authentic cultural knowledge of the language. It is more difficult to detect in material presented solely in graphic form; yet it is evident that misinterpretations of the right occasion or tone of voice for a certain expression can be a potent source of misunderstanding. At more advanced levels records, tape recordings, and films of native actors performing plays can be helpful.

The second type, the internal verbal context, or the implicit verbalization elicited by the sign, shows the attitude to the object. Certain words and expressions tend to occur in close association in the language, and these associations must be learned for full comprehension. Such associations can be acquired from much reading or listening to native speakers, or from "clichés" inserted in material for memorization. Familiarity with them leads to ease of communication and fluency in conversation.

The external nonverbal context, or total situational matrix, composed of facial expression and gestures of the speaker and the associated objects and activities, is the context most frequently neglected in foreign-language teaching. Unless the teacher has an intimate knowledge of the culture of the native speakers of the language, this context must be supplied by visual aids, particularly films made in the country where the language is spoken.

The external verbal context in which the sign is imbedded, sometimes called intraverbal context, is the context which is carefully analyzed by structural linguists. A knowledge of the structure of the language and familiarity with surrounding words can give many clues to meaning. Deductions made by the student in this way may often be inexact

---

[37] Osgood (1953), p. 725.

or even erroneous. When a word or expression has been met in a great variety of contexts, not purely intraverbal, first impressions may have to be re-examined and new deductions made. Most advocates of the audio-lingual method agree that sometimes an explanation or a gloss in the native language is necessary to avoid waste of time in later correction of misconceptions formed by inexperienced student deductions. Words learned through glosses or native-language equivalents come under the heading of what Osgood has called "assigns."[38] Assigns acquire their meaning through association with other signs, and so are more complicated than signs which derive their meaning from the direct experience of the individual, as they draw elements from representational mediation processes derived from several sources. When more research has been done in the area of "assigns," Osgood and his associates should have some interesting suggestions to make about the acquisition of cultural ideas through reading.

The implications of these four classes of context support the ideal of the active language classroom. Purely intraverbal context, as we have seen, can be very misleading, but when it is supported by facial expression, tone of voice, and contrived situation the clues are considerably increased. From the interplay of these factors a much more rounded conception of meaning is possible, particularly when the situation is planned to give cultural clues as well. The context is given an extra dimension where there is a give-and-take between individuals and an interested audience. Skinner has said that "an audience is a discriminative stimulus acting prior to the emission of a response . . . . Even though we possess [verbal] behavior in some strength, we remain silent until an audience appears. The problem of getting someone to respond verbally is often the problem of creating a suitable audience."[39] Similarly, an unsympathetic audience can inhibit a response, as so often happens with a nervous and embarrassed student in the foreign-language class.

---

[38] *Ibid.*, pp. 677–98.
[39] Skinner (1948), p. 50.

Even in native-language situations, persons who are otherwise quite voluble will be reduced to silence in an inhibiting atmosphere with an unsympathetic audience. Silence in the foreign-language class similarly is not always due to lack of flexible knowledge of the language, but may indicate that the student feels he "has nothing to say" in the circumstances. This points again to the necessity of creating a relaxed, uncritical, and sympathetic atmosphere in the classroom in order that students may be uninhibited in the production of foreign-language responses and feel free to express themselves on subjects of personal interest. Unless each student has had considerable practice in oral production of foreign-language responses, he will not be sensitive to the response-correlated stimuli or "feedback" from the four types of context, which make for fluent and appropriate response in a foreign-language situation.

For many students, the only opportunity for this type of active stimulation in the foreign language is in the classroom. But, as Skinner has pointed out, the speaker may be his own audience,[40] and so increase the relative strength of his verbal responses through his own efforts. Students whose opportunities for interchange of foreign-language responses are limited should be encouraged to talk to themselves frequently in the language, aloud if possible, and to read aloud from modern colloquial writings, particularly plays. In this way habits of co-ordination of meaning, structure, and physical production are built, with "feedback" from the proprioceptive and aural stimulation. This will make for greater facility in a face-to-face language situation.

Growing comprehension and a deepening apprehension of cultural meaning can be gained from wide reading where words are met in a variety of contexts. The student must first, however, be given some training in reading for direct comprehension, so that he will not need to decipher or translate as he reads. The audio-lingual sources advise that in the early stages the student should not read anything he has not already heard and repeated aloud. After an

---

40 Skinner (1957), pp. 179–80.

initial period, this can be broadened to the reading of material similar in vocabulary and content to what he has heard and then extended to more advanced literature carefully chosen for its authenticity, its standard of difficulty, and its intrinsic interest. Great care should be taken to see that the extracts chosen do not reinforce unfortunate stereotypes in the student's mind. This wide reading can do a great deal to extend the student's knowledge of structure, increase his vocabulary (particularly his passive or recognition vocabulary), and throw much light on "meaning" in the cultural and psychological sense of the word. Such an increase in language knowledge may occur without direct intention on the part of the reader, as a form of "latent" or "incidental" learning.

Much experimentation has gone into the question of latent learning, or "learning without awareness." Hilgard, after giving a detailed account of this experimentation, concludes, "There is no longer any doubt but that, under appropriate circumstances, latent learning is demonstrable."[41] McGeoch and Irion prefer to discuss "incidental learning," or "learning which apparently takes place without a specific motive or a specific formal instruction and set to learn the activity or material in question."[42] After a survey of experimental work in this field, they state that "though learning may occur without apparent motivation, actually the subject is set or directed toward parts of the material by reason of habitual modes of attack, interests, meaning, or by varied self-instructions. When we couple with these considerations the complex and subtle influences exercised by the behavior repertoire of the individual upon the fixation of new responses, together with the possible influence of spread of effect, each of which is a function of some motivating condition, the stage is set for the acceptance of the statement that incidental learning is only 'apparently' unmotivated."[43] This seems to cover the case of a student's learning valuable language skills and cultural "meanings" while ostensibly enjoying a play, short story,

---

[41] Hilgard (1956), p. 214.
[42] McGeoch and Irion (1952), pp. 210 ff.
[43] *Ibid.*, p. 215.

or novel in the foreign language. As soon as students have passed the early stages, they should be encouraged to read extensively and in this way to build up their knowledge of the language and its culturally determined "meanings" independently of classroom teaching.

XIII

FOR THE PRACTICAL TEACHER:
RECOMMENDATIONS

WHAT can the practical teacher take from this intensive study of psychological learning theory and apply to specific problems of foreign-language teaching? Scattered through the preceding chapters have been a number of suggestions and recommendations for the modification or improvement of audio-lingual techniques—recommendations which have emerged from consideration of the experimental work of several schools of psychological thought. These will now be summarized without further reference to learning theory.

Basic to the audio-lingual approach are pattern drills and the memorization of dialogues. As we have seen, these are suitable techniques for making foreign-language responses automatic at the manipulative level. Both provide direct practice of structures, mechanical associations, and expressions in common use in everyday speech. Carefully conducted, they enable the student to know almost immediately whether his response is correct and appropriate, thus giving him the opportunity to rectify it, either orally or mentally, before it becomes established as his habitual response. Composed in language which is of use in real-life situations, with expressions and structures repeated in a variety of contexts, they provide valuable exercise in the active use of the language for the give-and-take of communication.

In unskilled and unpracticed hands, however, these techniques may become tedious. Such a situation can be avoided if the following recommendations are carefully heeded.

Students should understand the rationale of the methods by which they are being taught. It is important that the teacher explain to the students why they are being asked to do so much drilling of structures and expressions, and that careful attention during drill periods will enable them to advance more rapidly toward their ultimate objective of speaking the language fluently. Such explanations help to create a set to learn by this method and an appreciation of the value of the activity. The alertness which this produces delays the onset of possible boredom and fatigue. Such an understanding of the different approach to learning which is required in the foreign-language class is all the more desirable because the students' experiences in other high-school classes do not involve much rote learning.

The amount of unrelieved and unremitting drill in class and laboratory should be considered carefully, since such practice does not automatically result in learning where human factors are involved. Drill and mimicry-memorization to the point of boredom become punishing and distasteful to the student, who will then seek a way of escape from this situation. Such avoidance may be physical, manifested in absence from class or laboratory session, or mental, the student continuing to repeat as demanded, even making mechanical variations of the pattern, but with his thoughts far away from the work in hand. Later, the use of these very phrases may immediately arouse associations of an unpleasant emotional kind, and active use of the foreign language will be inhibited.

In cases where boredom does not accompany long periods of drill, fatigue may. Such fatigue is emotional, rather than physical, but is just as real and painful to the student. It is frequently caused by keeping the student at the same type of task for long periods. As pure memorization and repetition of drills and of dialogues involves the same types of mental processes and overt activity, passing from one to the other cannot be considered a change in the nature of the task facing the student. When dialogues are broken into small sections for memorization, thus losing their meaningful continuity, memorization constitutes a rote-learning task, like the memorization of patterns in which the crucial element has not been explained. Fatigue from over-long repetition of the same type of activity may occur in laboratory sessions where the programming does not provide for variety or in the classroom. The solution in the case of the laboratory lies in thoughtful planning of the practice tape. In the classroom, the teacher must be sensitive to class reaction and prepared to change the type of activity at the first signs of fatigue. This does not mean a change from one set of materials to another involving the same kind of approach, but a change in the type of learning actually required, from active drill to practice in aural comprehension, for instance, or to a question-answer session on some aspect of the culture. The experienced teacher will be ready to change long before such signs appear, having planned a lesson with much variety of activity.

Many articles and books on pattern drill use such expressions as the necessity for the "overlearning" of responses, the continuing of drill to the point of "automatic response," and "saturation practice." In an actual teaching situation, such expressions must be interpreted with certain reservations if the method is not to be self-defeating. It has been demonstrated that there is a limit to the amount of repetition which is effective for learning, even with reinforcement. As we have seen, the effect may be decremental if repetition is continued to the point where fatigue creeps in. It has also been demonstrated that too much "overlearning" results in stereotyped behavior and loss of flexibility, so that, at more advanced stages, the student cannot vary these "overlearned" responses so as to communicate his "personal meaning."

The chief proponents of the audio-lingual method advocate that patterns encountered and learned by rote in dialogues should be practiced by various types of drills to a point of automatic response before a generalization or explanation of structure is given. This "generalization" then describes for the student what he has been doing. If this method is followed rigorously, it is possible for students to memorize, practice by rote, and be able to manipulate structures without being aware of the crucial element involved. Many experiments have shown that memory is aided by an understanding of what one is doing. If some explanation is not given, the student will work out his own rationale of what he is practicing, a rationale to which the teacher has no access if no discussion takes place, and which cannot therefore be corrected by the teacher if it is based on erroneous assumptions. A private explanation of this kind may well arise from the student's experiences with his own language and so cause a form of native-language interference. By analogy with the structure in his own language which he considers parallel to the one he is practicing, he may teach himself quite erroneous extensions of the structure to which he is being introduced.

Gestalt studies have clearly shown the value of understanding the whole pattern (that is, of the functions of the various parts in relation to each other within the whole), if learning is to be readily transferable to similar, but not identical, situations. Overlearning without explanation of the crucial element, or the function of the parts in the whole, can lead to reproduction of the structure or expression, exactly as it has been learned, in a situation where such a response is pertinent. Of the usefulness of such automatic responses, where appropriate, there can be no doubt. Such occasions, however, do not account for all real-life communication situations. Greater flexibility in the use of what has been learned will result if the student understands how the elements of the response can be adapted to variations in the situation.

The following procedure is recommended to achieve this greater flexibility. First, the structure or expression should be met several times in contexts where its relationship to the design of the language may be observed, and its meaning (structural, lexical, and social-cultural) inductively absorbed from its use in such varying situations. After several encounters of this type, the student should be asked to describe the function of the structure and its relationships as he has observed them, a brief explanation being given by the teacher if the student has misinterpreted this function. This generalization about the function of the structure draws the student's attention to the crucial element involved in the new pattern. After this brief analysis, the structure should be drilled by methods involving analogy. As the drill is now meaningful, and the students are participating with understanding, the effectiveness of the drill will be increased and consequently the time required to reach a stage of automatic response will be reduced. In this way, the student is less likely to reach the point of fatigue through prolonged repetitive activity and the structure which has been drilled will be more available for reproduction in or adaptation to a variety of situations because the function of the crucial element has been clearly understood.

If this recommended procedure is followed the student will know not only that a response is "right," but also in what way it is "right," and thus develop flexibility in language usage. Students who are always in a position where the "right" response is put in their mouths by the structuring of the situation, but who do not fully understand either the situation or the response, can often give a very impressive demonstration of glib fluency in the classroom but be quite at a loss if asked to express themselves in a real act of communication. When they discover that this glibness is not useful outside of their accustomed classroom situation, such students are often bitterly disappointed and discouraged, even feeling it futile to continue with their study of the language.

Important as it is to make clear to the student what he is doing, it is equally important to relate the drills to his own interests. With a little imagination, the teacher will be able to construct drills which make the student say the kinds of things which he would like to be saying, to relate the drills to situations in the student's life, and to introduce a touch of humor from time to time. Humor relaxes tension and regains attention which may be wavering. In this way, even drill sessions may be conducted in the relaxed atmosphere so essential to good foreign-language learning.

As many drill sessions take place in the language laboratory, it is as well to look at the few observations which have been made about the laboratory situation. The laboratory is not in itself an indispensable part of any method, being a teaching aid like films or television. Classes can be conducted along strictly audio-lingual lines in schools which have no laboratory. The development of electronic aids has, however, coincided with the emergence of the audio-lingual method, and it is indisputable that they have made the oral-aural approach more practicable by relieving the teacher of much of the tedium of repetitious drill with the same material in successive classes.

Reduction in the amount of drill in which the teacher participates with the student may well be an advantage to the teacher and a disadvantage to the student. As the laboratory does not provide a face-to-face situation, with its accompanying features of gesture, facial expression, tone of voice, and meaningful situation, new words and expressions practiced exclusively in the laboratory do not develop associations with situational stimuli. It is possible, therefore, that students who have practiced speaking in isolation in the laboratory booth will feel the same embarrassment and diffidence which inhibit foreign-language behavior for so many people when they find themselves in a communication situation, especially with native speakers. It is important that laboratory work should not be considered a substitute for, but rather auxiliary to, face-to-face communication situations contrived in the classroom.

Because the teacher is not participating actively in the drill session in the laboratory, he needs to give much thought to the taped material used. In the classroom, the sensitive teacher is alert to signs of fatigue or boredom from prolonged repetition of the same activity, and at a moment's notice, he can change the type of activity or introduce a short diversion. In the laboratory, this is far from easy. The teacher must anticipate and forestall the point of fatigue by preparing taped material with variety of activity and subject matter and exercises which have not already been repeated in class. The laboratory session will then pass quickly for the student because his attention is caught and held, without flagging. In this way, too, the student will not have time and attention to give to mischievous and destructive activities, and more efficient learning will take place because he is concentrating on what he is doing.

In most language laboratories, identical material is presented to all members of the class at the same time, so that each person is expected to learn at the same rate and each is allowed an identical number of seconds to give the response. This simplifies the work of the teacher directing the laboratory session, but it may result in boredom for the most intelligent and frustration for those unable to learn at the rate required.[1] Some teachers have tried to meet this situation by dividing each class into two or more levels and then providing material adapted in degree of difficulty and amount of repetition to the needs of each of these levels. A laboratory library system, where each student takes out the material he needs and proceeds at his own rate, would provide the ideal solution to this problem, but it is not always administratively feasible.

The language laboratory tape as it is usually constructed provides for the reinforcement of the student's response by allowing him to hear the correct version immediately after he has pronounced his own. This is theoretically sound, but it can result in reinforcement of incorrect pronunciation and intonation if certain aspects of the learning situation in the laboratory are not kept in mind. Without careful training, many students are unable to recognize the fine distinction between the correct sound of the voice on the tape and the sound they themselves have produced, or, if they do recognize the distinction, are uncertain what they should do to bring their faulty pronunciation closer to that of the native speaker. Students can be taught to discriminate fine distinctions of sound by

---

[1] F. Marty prefers a system where the student operates a pause button on the tape recorder or teaching machine and so regulates the length of the pause according to his own needs.

carefully devised exercises[2] and can be taught the mechanics of the production of sounds not found in their own language. Exercises in discrimination and production of the sounds most difficult for the speaker of this language, carefully supervised for immediate correction or reinforcement of the correct response, are essential if much incorrect pronunciation is not to be indorsed by inner approval on the part of the student himself, long before it has reached a stage acceptable to the teacher.

The psychological evidence in this study strongly supports careful monitoring of the work of the students in their booths by the teacher. This is needed to avoid the reinforcement of unacceptable responses which the student does not recognize as such, to stimulate the student to raise the standard which he himself finds acceptable for his work, and to prevent frustration for the weaker student who recognizes that his responses are poor but is at a loss to see how they can be improved.

With the audio-lingual as with other methods, a question of major importance which arises is the following: How can we bring students from the stage of facile repetition of learned phrases and patterns to the fluent expression of their own ideas in spontaneous communication? This requires training at a second level of language behavior. Pattern drill and dialogue memorization play their parts in the automatization of indispensable associations in the foreign language—subject-verb agreements, word order, sentence patterns, question forms, negatives, tense sequences, and the other intricacies of the design of the new language. If fluency in expressing one's own meaning is to be developed, practice must also be given in this skill. The student must have much practice in selecting structures and vocabulary which will enable him to enter into communication with another person as he would wish to do. This he will have difficulty in doing if he has not been trained to recognize the crucial element in material on which he has been drilled and to see the functional rela-

---

[2] P. Pimsleur, L. Mace, and E. Keislar, *Preliminary Discrimination Training in the Teaching of French Pronunciation*, N.D.E.A. Project SAE 8950 (Berkeley, Calif., 1961).

tionship of a new element to the other elements in the whole pattern. If he has been trained in this more analytic way, however, he will be able to use these structures independently of the specific context in which he first learned them.

Practice in selection will involve a certain amount of trial-and-error behavior on the student's part. The teacher must accept this as a preliminary stage of the important process of finding a solution by using all the resources available, and the teacher's approval will strengthen and consolidate the appropriate response when it is finally produced. The hesitancy which may accompany this process is not of itself an indication of insufficient knowledge of the language, as, even in natural communication of our thoughts in the native language, we hem and haw and do not always express ourselves in absolutely correct structures. Once past the banal exchange of phrases related to everyday activities, we pause to select the clearest way of conveying our thoughts to others.

In order to provide the best possible setting for the development of spontaneous communication in the language, the teacher must realize that the student cannot converse in the foreign language if he has nothing to communicate. He must want to communicate and must have some idea to express. Attention should be given to the structuring of situations in the classroom which reproduce as closely as possible the features of a real-life communication situation in the native language. This can be achieved only if the material which the student has memorized and repeated is closely related to his real-life interests, expressed in language which is appropriate to everyday circumstances, and repeated in contexts which are as meaningful as possible. The atmosphere should be relaxed and there must be no tensions between student and teacher, or student and student, if the spontaneous use of the language is not to be inhibited. The silence which falls over a social group in a native-language situation where individuals do not feel at ease with each other has nothing to do with ability to speak the language. Silences in a foreign-language classroom can easily result from similar tensions. Ability to communicate freely in the foreign language will be developed more quickly in a classroom where the students, at ease with the teacher and their classmates, are always actively involved and feel free to divert the conversational line of the lesson from time to time to areas of interest to them, provided that the interchange is consistently carried on in the foreign language. Communication in the foreign language then becomes an effective way of reaching a goal: of obtaining the attention of teacher and classmates, of sharing ideas and interests, of obtaining further information, or of teasing one's friends. The effort to communicate in the foreign language is facilitated by give-and-take among peers and the presence of a sympathetic audience which is not unduly critical. In this way each student may have frequent experiences of success, in a major or minor form, and this feeling of success will increase his motivation to persist in the study of the language to a point of greater mastery.

With training of this nature in the classroom, the student will gain confidence from experience in communication in the foreign language and will not therefore suffer from embarrassment and inhibitions when face to face with a native speaker. As he will associate pleasant and successful experiences with the speaking of the language, he will be very ready to use it whenever possible. Above all, he will develop an adventurous attitude to the use of the language which will lead him into situations providing valuable practice beyond mere "school work," and he will advance rapidly as his own teacher, a stage which must eventually be reached by all who would attain genuine mastery of another language.

If the student is to be taught to speak the foreign language in a way which will communicate his own meaning to the native speakers of that language, he must learn more than structures and vocabulary. He must learn to share in the experiences which native speakers associate with vocabulary and expressions. Ideally, this would involve plunging each student for a certain period into the active life of a community which speaks the language. As this is possible for very few of our students, the teacher must be conscious of the fact that words and expressions of the foreign language isolated from a cultural context can give false impressions of meaning, and, if learned in this way, can prove to be very poor tools of communication with a native speaker. The teacher should see that materials he uses are culturally authentic and that the student is surrounded as much as possible by pictures, magazines, news items, films, music, songs, and other aids to understanding the life and ways of thought of the people who speak the language.

One of the most controversial tenets of the proponents of the audio-lingual method has been their insistence on withholding the graphic symbol—the printed or written word—from students in the early stages of learning a foreign language until the work has been thoroughly learned orally. Different recommendations are given by various leaders, ranging from withholding the script for a period of months to deferring it for several lessons. In this way it is hoped to avoid the interference of native-language habits associated with the familiar symbols. Experienced teachers[3] point out that this interference will occur in any case, at whatever stage the graphic form of the language is admitted to the classroom, and will have to be combated with constant vigilance.

This study has shown that making the student depend on aural signals alone in the early stages of learning a foreign language puts a much greater strain on the student than is generally realized. He is expected to hear clearly and retain every element of the material presented aurally in order to be able to reproduce it accurately. This is more than he actually does in his native language. In a native-language situation, he hears certain syntactic and associational cues and recognizes the context from environmental cues. In this way he is able to supply what he does not hear clearly. Because the student is not in a position to recognize such cues in the foreign language, a lengthy period when material is presented in an aural form only can arouse tensions within him which may prevent him

---

[3] See quotation from Fernand Marty in chap. x, pp. 111–12.

from organizing and retaining what he has heard. This is particularly so at the high-school level, where the student has had some six or seven years of training in drawing his information from written material or noting it down in written form for future reference. To relieve these tensions, many students will surreptitiously make notes, which are frequently erroneous, or will develop their own visual images of what they are repeating, images which are inaccessible to the teacher and so may also perpetuate error.

This period of purely aural-oral work is particularly trying for students with poor auditory discrimination or a nervous or anxious temperament, who feel insecure when forced to depend on the ear alone. In the early stages such students may develop an aversion to foreign-language study which will affect later attitudes. They may also fall so far behind their fellows that they feel frustrated, embarrassed, and humiliated.

As the problem of native-language interference through the use of the graphic symbol will have to be faced at some stage, it might as well be in the early stages so that the student can have a longer period of association of correct sound with written symbol. To reduce the amount of interference, the teacher should never allow students in the early stages to attempt to read material which they have not already heard pronounced orally, or which they are not simultaneously hearing as they read it silently. With this safeguard, and constant vigilance on the part of the teacher, the script can be of immense help in reducing the student's dependence on the teacher. It will give the student something to which to refer when his aural memory fails him, thus giving him greater confidence in his oral work.

This recommendation that the graphic symbol be available to the student does not mean that the teacher may not present new material aurally with books closed. Such a procedure provides valuable training in depending on the ear alone, training which the high-school student certainly needs. It is also valuable as a way of focusing attention on pronunciation and intonation and their improvement. The material should, however, be seen and practiced with aural and visual stimuli in association, before students are expected to memorize it. This will shorten the time required for memorization and allow more class time for use of the material in a variety of ways in order to make it a part of the student's repertoire. However, it should not shorten the time spent on active use of the material, as this is the most worthwhile activity of the foreign-language classroom if present objectives are to be achieved.

When the student has become familiar with basic structures and vocabulary, he should be encouraged to do much wide reading of authentic materials in order to increase his familiarity with the culture and ways of thinking of the community who speak the language. Much reading will also greatly increase the student's passive or recognition vocabulary and familiarity with idiomatic expression. If such reading is to be effective in building concepts of meaning equivalent to those of the native speaker, and in increasing the student's desire to know even more of the language and the culture it embodies, the materials must be selected so as not to reinforce unfavorable stereotypes and prejudices which many students already possess when they approach the study of another culture. Students with unfavorable attitudes toward the native speakers of a language do not advance as rapidly in the study of that language as do those with favorable attitudes. Materials should not present the odd and unusual, the socially deviant, the old-fashioned and peculiarly regional, unless it is made clear to the students that these do not represent the life of a person of equivalent social standing to himself in a contemporary society. Later, they may be read for their intrinsic interest as they would be in the native language.

The study of the way language is learned has brought out the fact that a strong emotional element is involved. As we express our personality through speech and its associated features, the student who is asked to begin learning a foreign language is placed in a completely different position from that in which he finds himself in any other school subject. We are suddenly depriving him of a support and a defense, of a tool for inquiry, self-expression, and retention.

If the student dislikes the teacher, he will resent his dependence on him in the foreign-language class. The teacher who would succeed in teaching a foreign language must be conscious of the invidious, frustrating, and insecure position in which the student finds himself in the early stages and must be able to inspire confidence through his understanding and patience. He must be sensitive to the emotional reactions of the students, to signs of nervousness and anxiety, and to indications of embarrassment and even of antagonism toward the subject,[4] being quick to take steps to eliminate such undesirable manifestations of inner tension. He must also be sensitive to the interplay of personalities in the classroom if he is to develop the relaxed atmosphere of give-and-take which is essential if students are to have practice in spontaneous communication in the foreign language.

It is particularly important for the teacher to realize that the motivation of each student in the class is not, at the beginning, intrinsic to the subject. By seeking to understand the forces motivating the student, and the level of aspiration which he has as a consequence set himself, the teacher will be able to work to change this motivation where necessary, and to lead the student to see different goals as rewarding and desirable. When he approaches the student in this way, he will understand that reinforcement of correct responses is not an automatic process, equivalent for all his students. He will seek, then, to reinforce responses and attitudes in accordance with the individual student's perceived goals.

As the teacher expresses his personality through language just as much as the student, he should employ methods and use materials in the way which makes him feel most relaxed and spontaneous. This will enable him to use his imagination in developing all the language skills and in bringing variety into each lesson. When he is relaxed, he will be more sensitive to all the indications of interest or tedium, of confidence or insecurity, of eagerness to contribute an original element or desire to work unidentified in the group,

---

[4] The reasons for these reactions and the fatigue and inhibition which they can cause are discussed fully in chap. ix.

and be ready to adapt his prepared material to meet these needs. Similarly he will be conscious of different rates of learning and provide for these in laboratory and classroom.

Keating's report on the effectiveness of language laboratories has brought out the fact that a good foreign-language teacher without a language laboratory is able to achieve better results with his students than a teacher who has the help of a laboratory, especially after the first year.[5] This is perhaps not so much a criticism of the use of language laboratories as such as an indication of the widespread misuse of them by untrained teachers unsure of how to integrate the work of the laboratory into the general language program. Be that as it may, it does support the general thesis of this book that language communication involves a relationship between individuals and not merely the memorization and repetition of phrases and the practicing of structures. As Hjelmslev has observed, "It is in the nature of language to be overlooked, to be a means and not an end."[6] Fluent foreign-language use is a means of reaching out beyond national boundaries in the expression of ideas and personality, and in the comprehension of them— a skill and an art which our twentieth-century world requires of as many of its citizens as possible. With a full awareness of the human factors involved, the sensitive teacher will adopt and adapt techniques according to his own personality and those of his students, so that the foreign-language lesson becomes a living experience of communication, rather than another tedious class hour.

---

[5] Keating (1963), p. 39. The research involved schools in districts which could employ superior teachers.

[6] Hjelmslev (1961), p. 5.

APPENDIX
THEORIES OF LEARNING

IN ORDER to understand the positions held by modern learning theorists and the terms they use to describe the learning process, it may be helpful to trace their development from their original roots in earlier theories and experimental research.

Frequently the same term will be used by different psychologists with a slightly different intention. The deeper significance of the term becomes clearer as we read the story of the development of the concept. Certain controversies must be understood, controversies unresolved on present experimental evidence, which may be interpreted from differing theoretical positions and for which it is often difficult to devise a crucial experiment that clearly isolates the element at issue.

Living organisms are so complex that many unexpected factors may enter in. For this reason, psychologists often return to earlier experiments, reproducing them under conditions as nearly similar as possible, to see if the same results will be obtained. If an experiment is valid, it should be possible to reproduce the same results under the same experimental conditions. If the outcome is different, some unidentified factor has probably been at work which would necessitate the drawing of a different conclusion.

Certain theorists try to work out a synthesis of the controversial facts and thus act as a bridge between schools of thought. As more facts emerge and incontrovertible laws can be established, psychology should become more unified; but the present divergent schools do valuable work by extending the horizons of research in the area of their particular emphasis. Adherents of the various schools of thought do not remain in water-tight compartments but examine the research of others, endeavoring to throw light on it from their differing theoretical viewpoints.

It was not until the latter part of the nineteenth century that psychology became an experimental science,[1] in the present-day sense of the term, under such pioneers as Wilhelm Wundt in Germany and William James at Harvard. As psychology was considered to be the science of states of consciousness, or conscious experience, the accepted method of research at that time was the *method of introspection*, with careful controls established, in order to insure that the data obtained should be as objective and scientific as possible. Under the influence of Darwinian theory, however, psychologists soon became interested in the way the individual adapts to his environment. These early psychologists were not yet actively interested in experimental research into how an organism learns; they accepted the viewpoint of the British associationists, in the tradition of Hobbes, Hume, and Hartley, that ideas developed from the linking together of sensations which occurred simultaneously or in rapid succession. At the turn of the century the major step forward in the study of the learning process took place, when Thorndike and Pavlov independently discovered the *law of "effect"* or *"reinforcement"* and set off a long train of research, mainly with animals, into the processes involved in learning.

THORNDIKE AND THE LAW OF EFFECT[2]

During a long career in psychology, Thorndike's thinking passed through various stages, his earlier ideas being modified by later experimentation. His most important contribution is his famous Law of Effect, which states that if an act is followed by a satisfying state of affairs the probability of its recurrence in a similar situation is increased. The satisfying state of affairs has a quality of "belongingness" or appropriateness. It either satisfies an aroused motive or want in the learner or provides information about the results of certain actions.

---

[1] Woodworth (1948), chaps. i-iii.
[2] Hilgard (1956), chap. ii.

The first appearance of the act which is ultimately learned is the result of trying out various possible responses to a stimulus situation until one proves to be appropriate. This type of performance is commonly called *trial-and-error behavior,* but Thorndike preferred to call it learning by *selecting and connecting.* The organism has a total attitude or "set" toward a goal that influences the selection it makes, this selection being based partly on previous experience and partly on inborn tendencies. To Thorndike, associations were "connections" between situation and response, and his system came to be called Connectionism.

Thorndike also propounded the law of *associative shifting,* by which a response that continues through a number of fundamental changes in the stimulating situation may eventually be elicited by a completely different stimulus. We shall see as we proceed that these ideas are not unlike the notions of reinforcement and the conditioned stimulus which were to grow out of interest in the research of the Russian physiologist, Pavlov.

Thorndike was also interested in the question of *transfer* of what has been learned to a new situation. His research led him to the conclusion that transfer takes place when there are identical elements of substance or procedure in the original learning and in the new situation. In this way learning is specific and it is specific connections which are reusable.

PAVLOV AND THE CONDITIONED REFLEX[3]

Pavlov, who was a physiologist and not a psychologist, made his important discovery of the conditioned reflex while studying salivary reflexes in dogs. He discovered that after a number of occasions when a certain phenomenon (e.g., the ticking of a metronome) had preceded the placing of food in a dog's mouth, the salivary reflex, which is a natural reflex in response to food in the mouth, would appear in response to the ticking of the metronome. This

---

[3] Woodworth (1948), pp. 56–63; Hilgard (1956), pp. 50–51.

learned reflex he called the *conditioned reflex* (CR), and the abnormal stimulus which aroused it was called the *conditioned stimulus* (CS). The food was the *unconditioned stimulus,* as it would normally arouse the salivary reflex (the *unconditioned reflex*), and this unconditioned stimulus came to be referred to as the *reinforcement.* If the reinforcement were not supplied during a number of trials, then ultimately the conditioned reflex would cease to appear. This process was called *extinction.* Pavlov also found that the conditioned reflex could be aroused by stimuli similar to, but not identical with, the conditioned stimulus, and this process was called *stimulus generalization.* By differential reinforcement (that is, presenting and withholding reinforcement according to a particular pattern) the animal could be trained to make finer and finer distinctions between similar stimuli and would learn to respond only to those which had been reinforced. This process was called *differentiation* (later *conditioned discrimination*). After a period of rest, responses which had been subject to extinction would tend to recur, and this was called *spontaneous recovery.* If reinforcement were still not forthcoming, these responses would be subject to fairly rapid extinction and would disappear altogether from the animal's repertoire.

In Pavlov's experiments, the conditioned stimulus did not appear at the same time as the unconditioned stimulus but always shortly before it, thus arousing the conditioned reflex before the unconditioned reflex. The conditioned reflex was never exactly the same as the unconditioned reflex but rather took the form of a preparatory response, being a new form of response rather than an appearance of the unconditioned reflex. Unlike Thorndike's response which is strengthened by reinforcement, Pavlov's CR was not instrumental in obtaining reinforcement for the animal, since the reinforcement was given automatically whether the CR occurred or not. This Pavlovian situation shows the pattern of what is called *classical conditioning.* Thorndike's learned response was more akin to what has come to be known as *instrumental or operant conditioning,* this being the main area of research of B. F. Skinner.

ORIGINS OF BEHAVIORISM[4]

Pavlov's experiments became familiar to Americans at a time when psychology was undergoing a revolution. Led by Watson, the new movement was called behaviorism, because it took as its chief study the observed behavior of the organism rather than some unobservable inner process determining that behavior. Its main tenet, that psychology must limit itself to the study of the objectively observable, has profoundly influenced psychological experiment to this day. The environmental stimulus (i.e., the sum of stimuli acting on the sense organs at a given time) is observable, and the response is observable as it impinges on the environment. Since introspection is rejected as a method of objective investigation, what takes place between stimulus and response is not considered the province of the behavioral psychologist, unless it can be directly observed as muscle movement, glandular secretion, or other measurable bodily change. Because of the restriction of its interest to stimulus and response, behaviorism became known as *S-R psychology*.

The early behaviorists were soon studying Pavlov's work with conditioned reflexes and their accompanying processes, and using this work as a basis for much of their experimentation. As they broadened their study from reflexes to other forms of behavior they began to speak of *conditioned responses* to conditioned stimuli. Rejecting as they did the method of introspection and being determined to keep to what was overtly observable, the behaviorists began to lay great emphasis on the study of animal behavior as a more fundamental form which would be shown to follow the same basic laws as human behavior.

GUTHRIE'S CONTIGUOUS CONDITIONING[5]

E. R. Guthrie, whose approach is behavioristic, rejected the necessity for reinforcement in favor of contiguity, stating that a response which occurred in the presence of a combination of stimuli would tend to recur in a situation where these stimuli were reproduced. Reward or a

---

[4] Woodworth (1948), pp. 69–94; Hilgard (1956), pp. 48–50.
[5] Hilgard (1956), chap. iii.

satisfying state of affairs did not, he believed, increase the probability of a preceding response being repeated but did reduce the possibility of other responses occurring in the presence of the existing stimuli, thus preserving the response in the form in which it had occurred. The response is actually learned in one trial, a skill being composed of a large number of habits acquired in this way.

The real stimuli which condition responses are the *movement-produced stimuli* experienced by the organism, and these explain similar responses which apparently occur in response to different stimuli. To develop a habit in an individual it is necessary to arrange the situation so that certain movements will take place in the presence of certain cues. On the reappearance of these cues the same behavior will tend to recur. Practice attaches cues to movements, and in the development of a complex skill many different cues must be attached to the appropriate movement. *Extinction* is brought about by causing new movements to occur in the presence of the cues which originally stimulated the undesired behavior. It is evident that in the development of a habit, according to this theory, movements must be practiced in the precise form which will later be required. In other words, *we learn what we do*. Highly desirable behavior should be practiced in the presence of as many stimulus supports as possible, so that it will recur despite distraction and competing tendencies. In taking this position, Guthrie was closer to Watson's views than the other behaviorist psychologists to be discussed, who, like B. F. Skinner, retained and developed the concept of reinforcement or reward as an essential element in learning or habit formation.

TOLMAN'S PURPOSIVE BEHAVIORISM OR EXPECTANCY THEORY[6]

A different type of behaviorism emerged with E. Tolman, who called himself a "purposive behaviorist." To him, behavior was not adequately described from the *"molecular"* point of view (i.e., in terms of its strict underlying physical

---

[6] Woodworth (1948), pp. 103–8; Hilgard (1956), chap. vi.

and physiological details), but had *"molar"* qualities (i.e., each component of behavior must be viewed as part of a larger picture of behavior which is goal-directed or purposive). To Tolman, what an animal learns is not an act but a means to an objectively determinable end. By what appears to be trial-and-error behavior, the animal explores the situation until it finds the way that will lead to the goal. Some of this preliminary behavior is observed to be systematic in the elimination of possible approaches to the goal, and much of it is based on previous experience. The animal thus has a *goal expectancy* that influences its behavior. Tolman conducted most of his experiments with a maze type of apparatus in which the animal had to find its way to the goal, or reward, despite various obstacles.

Tolman also introduced the concept of *intervening variables* between stimulus and response. These are variables which must be taken into consideration in describing behavior; they are not observable but may be inferred from objectively observed behavior. Intervening variables are not mentalistic but may be such things as appetite, physical needs, motor skill, or such cognitive elements as hypotheses about means to the goal. These hypotheses are confirmed by success in achieving the goal. Success is considered by Tolman not to reinforce the behavior but to confirm the expectancy of the animal, and thus to increase the probability of recurrence of this behavior. In this way a *positive cathexis* or attraction is established between the initial drive and the goal-object. This cathexis increases the energy put into the behavior in relation to the goal-object.

Tolman believed that some of his experiments showed the animal to be capable of *latent learning*. During an exploratory period, he considered that it learned certain things about its environment which enabled it at a later stage, when so motivated, to find the shortest route to the goal. He also observed that at a choice point the animal would stop and make exploratory movements with its head as though comparing stimuli, before setting out on a route. This he called *vicarious trial-and-error* behavior, or VTE, and maintained that it indicated perceptual and cognitive processes controlling behavior. As we shall see in a later section, this draws close to Gestalt thinking.

HULL'S SYSTEMATIC DRIVE-REDUCTION THEORY[7]

C. Hull set out to develop a theory of behavior based on Pavlov's laws of conditioning. He wished to establish a system with definite laws, logically deduced, which could be tested by experiment. In this way psychology would become a science which could predict behavior as well as describe it. He included in his system Tolman's concept of *intervening variables* and his distinction between molecular and molar behavior.

Hull was primarily interested in *habit formation* and accepted the idea that reinforcement is of basic importance. The most important of his intervening variables is *drive,* and reinforcement is considered to be effective in forming habits because it *reduces drive.* Drives are tension states which energize the organism; they are based on physical needs, such as hunger and thirst, which are satisfied by *primary reinforcement* in the form of food and water. Later, under the influence of Neal Miller, Hull moved to the position that reduction of the intensity of the stimuli associated with the drive is as reinforcing as the actual reduction of the drive (thus food in the mouth does not reduce hunger, but it is reinforcing as it *reduces the drive-stimulus* or craving for food). This leads to the concept of *secondary reinforcement,* in that things which are not actually drive- or need-reducing, but which are consistently associated with the things which reduce the stimuli associated with the drive, can become reinforcing through this association and themselves reduce drive-stimuli. Similarly, things which are consistently associated with drive-stimuli can acquire power to arouse a *secondary drive,* such as anxiety or fear. Learning is considered to be a consequence of either primary or secondary reinforcement, but the strength of a response depends on the level of drive (or drives) which is operating at that particular moment. Failure to act may be due to

---

[7] Hilgard (1956), chap. v.

reactive inhibition which results from pain or fatigue and acts either as a barrier to repetition of the act or as a drive strengthening any activity associated with its reduction, such as rest. As in the Pavlovian system, Hull and Miller speak of stimulus *generalization,* stimulus *discrimination, extinction,* and *spontaneous recovery.* Alternative ways of acting in relation to the goal are drawn together by an inferred integrating mechanism, or intervening variable, called a *fractional, antedating goal reaction* which provides a stimulus to which all the overt responses are conditioned and which is therefore present when any of these responses takes place. If one of these responses is strengthened, then the other members of the *habit family* are strengthened and their reaction potential is also increased. The responses in the family form a *hierarchy,* those closest to the goal being the strongest. This particular intervening variable (the fractional, antedating goal reaction) is regarded by many of Hull's critics as a very elastic concept which is not rigorously defined.

K. Spence[8] has examined this theory of Hull's and has concluded that reinforcement does not strengthen instrumental responses (these are strengthened because they occur), but it does strengthen these fractional, antedating goal responses so that *incentive motivation* is increased, making the organism want to repeat the act. Thus the strength, or probability of recurrence, of the instrumental response is increased, but not merely as habit strength. In cases of *frustration,* this incentive motivation will actually increase drive strength, exciting the organism to activity. Thus the fractional, antedating goal responses take on a mediating function.

Neal Miller[9] has developed the concept of *acquired* (or *secondary*) *drives* in human subjects which are learned rather than innate. Paralleling the primary drive of pain, for instance, is the learned or secondary drive of fear or anxiety. As the individual grows older, he acquires many

---

[8] Spence (1956), pp. 133–37.
[9] N. Miller (1941).

social attitudes which replace primary drives but which were originally associated with primary need states. Various social drives are generated which greatly influence human behavior, such as gregariousness, social conformity, desire for money, and imitativeness. Once acquired, they operate exactly like primary drives. Relief of an acquired drive is an acquired reward or reinforcement and therefore *secondary reinforcement*.

The problem of new learning will often have to be solved by placing the individual in a *learning dilemma*. As long as habitual responses are rewarded, the individual is unlikely to try new responses by trial and error as his drive level remains low. If, however, he is placed in a situation where his habitual responses do not bring reward, he will be forced to try new responses and so learn new behavior. This is particularly relevant to a teaching situation.

Learning to respond to similar classes of cues in different circumstances is called by Miller *abstraction*. It involves recognizing the crucial element which is similar in each context. As the response is always rewarded when the crucial element is present, the response becomes more and more strongly connected with the relevant cue and extinguished as a response to other cues. In this way a weak stimulus may come to have an *acquired cue value*.

An individual may learn to generalize from one situation to another which has no external cues in common with the first. Such generalization can be *mediated* by *response-produced cues* (i.e., there is a common response to both situations which produces cues which can serve as the stimuli necessary for generalization). Such response-produced cues, for instance those associated with verbal responses, play an important part in social behavior, and stimuli associated with verbal responses may even acquire drive value and thus provoke action.

Speech can become an anticipatory response, becoming more and more abbreviated, and thus plays an important role in thinking and reasoning. The sequence of cue-producing responses employed in reasoning is often learned by the individual as part of his culture.

Skinner's Operant Conditioning[10]

For the past twenty-five years, one of the most important figures on the psychological scene has been B. F. Skinner, whose name has become associated with one of the commonest types of experimental apparatus, the Skinner box.

Skinner has consistently espoused the strict behaviorist position of drawing psychological conclusions only from the physically observable. He has not interested himself to any degree in the physiological side of behavior (the role of the nervous system, glands, or muscles). He has devoted himself essentially to the study of stimulus-response units and their relationship to other experimental variables, such as intensity of stimulus, number of trials, amount of reinforcement.

Skinner divides behavior into *respondent behavior,* where a known stimulus elicits a response, and *operant behavior,* where a spontaneous response is emitted for which the stimulus is not known, or at least is not under the control of the experimenter. Parallel to this, he speaks of two types of conditioning, Type S and Type R. Type S represents the conditioning of respondent behavior, where the reinforcement is natural and correlated with the stimuli (hence the use of the letter S), and it follows the classical conditioning (Pavlovian) paradigm. According to Skinner, Type S is rarely found in the pure form and is not very important. Type R (where the response is correlated with reinforcement) is what Skinner calls *operant or instrumental conditioning.* This, he says, produces the commonest form of behavior, and it has been the chief center of interest of his experimental research.

Operant Conditioning

In operant conditioning, the reinforcement is contingent on the response of the organism. This conditioned response is not related in any natural way to the form of the reinforcing stimulus which it causes to appear, and it does not resemble the natural response to this reinforcing stimulus.

---

[10] Hilgard (1956), chap. iv; Woodworth (1948), pp. 63–66, 112–16; Skinner (1957).

This is best illustrated by a description of the Skinner box, which was designed for the investigation of this type of behavior.

The *Skinner box* is a small, bare area with a little tin pan in one corner and a mechanism outside for dropping pellets of food into the pan. As each pellet drops into the pan it makes a pinging sound which attracts the rat's attention to the food in the pan. After the rat has become accustomed to being fed in this way, a small lever is introduced into the box. When the rat accidentally presses this lever, a pellet falls with a ping into the dish. Very soon the rat learns to press the bar whenever it is hungry. This apparatus can then be used for a number of different experiments by varying the experimental conditions. The appearance of the food, *the reinforcing stimulus,* is contingent on the action of the animal, the *conditioned response,* yet lever-pressing has no natural connection with the appearance of food, nor does it resemble the natural response to the appearance of food (salivating, approach movements). The conditioned response is operant or instrumental, in that it causes the food to appear. In this way Type R is quite distinct from Type S conditioning, where the conditioned response is an anticipatory, weaker variety of the natural, unconditioned response (e.g., salivating in the Pavlovian experiments), and where the appearance of the reinforcing stimulus is not brought about by the conditioned response.

Operant or instrumental behavior therefore has an effect upon the environment which rewards the organism which emits the response. Whether this response (e.g., lever-pressing) is emitted in the first place as the result of trial-and-error behavior, selecting and connecting, or insight is of no interest to Skinner, who has concentrated on observing what happens after the response has been emitted and what conditions increase the probability of its recurrence, which is the measure of its *operant strength.* In this way, Skinner defines his variables operationally. Hunger, for instance, is defined as hours of deprivation. It therefore becomes an observable and quantifiable variable, and any kind of empathy in the description of its effect is avoided. Learning is demonstrated by an increase in the rate of responding, which is an indication of the increased probability of response. Skinner therefore prefers to use the term "increase of operant strength," rather than "learning." At no stage does Skinner use terms like motivation, incentive, or purpose, which could be interpreted as attributing mentalistic qualities to the organism under observation, nor does he presume the existence of any intervening variables, like drive, which cannot be observed objectively.

Reinforcement

As a result of his experimentation with animals, Skinner has come to the conclusion that reinforcement always increases the probability of recurrence of a response. The response must occur before it can be reinforced, and reinforcement is most effective if it is prompt and occurs before any other behavior can intervene. Withholding of reinforcement leads eventually to extinction of the particular response, but the more reinforcements the animal has experienced, the more resistant to extinction does the learned response become.

Skinner has also experimented with different rates and intervals of reinforcement and has found that *variable-interval reinforcement* produces a stable response which is highly resistant to extinction because there is a strong probability of reinforcement at any moment. He has also shown experimentally the reality of spontaneous recovery of a response in the process of extinction after a period of rest, the weakening of a response as reinforcement is withheld, the generalization of responses so that they tend to occur in the presence of similar stimuli, and the possibility of teaching finer and finer discriminations among similar stimuli by differential reinforcement.

His experiments with the conditioning of "superstitious" behavior in pigeons are famous. In these experiments, accidental responses happening at the time of reinforcement (e.g., neck-stretching and half-turns) are repeated by the pigeons although they are irrelevant to the obtaining of food. Working on such accidental occurrences, by careful giving and withholding of reinforcement, he has been able to lead the pigeons, through successive approximations, to the pattern of behavior he had in mind, thus teaching them to accomplish whole series of complicated responses. Basic to this type of training, already familiar to animal trainers, is the fact that the animal tends to repeat what it was doing at the time of reinforcement.

Recently, Skinner has become interested in human learning. He believes that fundamental learning processes are the same in animals and in men, and he has been applying his principles of learning through reinforcement to the development of teaching machines. In this case, the reinforcement is *secondary reinforcement,* which Skinner believes plays a major role in human behavior. Secondary reinforcers, like praise, money, and social acceptance, have acquired their power to reinforce social behavior by repeated association with primary reinforcers, such as food. Through conditioning, they have acquired the power to condition. By the process of generalization, many other stimuli acquire this secondary conditioning power.

In the teaching-machine situation, the secondary reinforcer is the immediate knowledge of results, of whether one is right or wrong. The program in the teaching machine breaks the material to be learned into its smallest elements. Responses to questions based on these minimal steps are rewarded or punished immediately by the knowledge of success or failure and thus are reinforced and rendered more liable to recur. In this way a whole body of knowledge is learned. What is known about the most favorable schedules of reinforcement can also be worked into the machines.

Verbal Behavior

Skinner has also turned his attention to the distinctive feature of man's behavior: speech, which he calls verbal behavior. According to Skinner verbal behavior is emitted behavior which is reinforced by a listener and develops according to the same principles as other operant behavior. In certain circumstances the speaker becomes his own listener and reinforces his own verbal behavior. Just as Skinner is not interested in what may cause a response to be emitted in ordinary behavior, so he limits himself to the observable in verbal behavior, considering notions of "meaning" and "intention" to be mentalistic and outside the province of the scientific psychologist unless they can be defined operationally and examined as objectively as other forms of behavior.

GESTALT PSYCHOLOGY[11]

Another important movement in modern psychology, which is quite distinct from behaviorism, is the Gestalt school. This school dates from the association of Wertheimer, Koffka, and Köhler in Germany in the early part of the twentieth century and it has devoted a great deal of attention to perceptual processes, producing a body of experimentation different from that of the behaviorists. Much of the work has been with human subjects. Unlike the behaviorists, the Gestalt group did not reject the method of introspection as a source of information. They also felt that much of the significance of behavior was lost in the examination of small elements like S-R units. To them a whole act has a significance which gives meaning to its parts, and it is from this emphasis that the school developed its name. A *"gestalt"* is a form, and there is a form which is present in a whole which is lost when the parts are examined in detail without reference to their relationship to the whole. Rearranged, the parts make up a different whole which has a different form or "gestalt." This is clearly illustrated in the notes which make up a musical tune. It was Ehrenfels in Austria who first called attention to this "gestalt" quality, or *form quality,* and founded the Austrian Gestalt school. The name was taken up by the new group in Germany, which became known as the Berlin Gestalt school. These psychologists of the Berlin group later came to the United States. They did not go as far as the Austrian Gestalt group in looking for a higher mental process at work in the perception of wholes but maintained that the sensory process organized what was perceived into patterns. This *organization* which took place was influenced by past experience, so that people "recognized" and identified

---

[11] Woodworth (1948), chap. v; Hilgard (1956), chap. vii.

certain objects or groups of objects. Through their study of the organization of perception, the Gestalt psychologists were able to formulate *laws or principles of organization*.

The first of these laws is the *Law of Prägnanz* or good figure. In perceiving an object, our senses tend to organize it so that its "gestalt" has regularity, symmetry, and simplicity. Irregularities are leveled out and normalized. This process is aided by familiarity, or a "set" to see it in a certain way. Subordinate to this law of good figure are the four laws of *similarity, proximity, closure,* and *good continuation*. Similar items tend to form groups, as do those nearest to each other. We tend in perception to complete what is incomplete, just as in behavior we tend toward a situation which is completed and feel tension until it has reached some conclusive stage. This is the law of closure, which may be considered as the Gestalt equivalent of the Law of Effect. The reduction of tension which comes with closure is satisfying, as is reinforcement or reward. Good continuation refers to the fact that we perceive things in a way which shows them fitting together in a well-articulated, stable group.

Koffka moved further into the general area of human behavior, developing a theory that man moves in a *"behavioral environment"* which is structured according to his own experiences of the interacting forces within him and outside of him. Each "behavioral environment" is different from that of others; each person responds to the environment as he perceives it and as it is shaped by his interests, needs, and abilities.

Gestalt psychologists were not primarily interested in learning, but felt that the laws of organization in perception were applicable to learning.

Wertheimer made a study of "Productive Thinking"[12] in which he emphasized the necessity in learning for the student to go beyond the parts learned by repetition and drill to an understanding of the structure of the whole and the function of each part in this structure. The student, he said, must not blindly follow a formula but must under-

---

[12] Wertheimer (1945).

stand what he is doing. Problems to be solved are gaps which must be closed according to the principles of organization at work in the whole.

Köhler, who experimented a great deal with apes, was also interested in problem-solving, and maintained that the solution of the problem came at a moment of *"insight"* when the animal perceived the parts to have a relationship. Intelligence and prior experience made insightful solutions more probable. Köhler objected to the S-R formula as the unit of behavior, maintaining that between the stimulus and response are organizational processes that affect the nature of the response. The right psychological formula to him would be: pattern of stimulation—organization—response to the products of organization. Consequently, what may be called trial-and-error behavior is not fortuitous fumbling but represents the trying-out of preliminary hypotheses that emerge from the structuring of the field as perceived by the individual. Many of these hypotheses will be incorrect until the individual "sees" the problem as a whole and the parts in relation to the whole. Then his response will take account of this organization.

Katona[13] applied this same theoretical framework to his interpretation of his experiments on learning. He decided that the method of *"direct practice,"* or repetitive drill where understanding is not required, is effective where specific elements of the learning situation will be reproduced in later situations exactly as they have been learned. This includes rules learned by rote. The *understanding* of a principle, of the whole qualities of a situation, and of the relationship between the parts, on the other hand, leads to better application of the learning in situations which are physically different. This is the Gestalt approach to transfer of training, called *transposition,* and it complements Thorndike's identical elements transfer.

LEWIN'S FIELD THEORY[14]

Another psychologist who began his career in association with the Berlin Gestalt group is Kurt Lewin. Lewin, how-

---

[13] Katona (1940).
[14] Hilgard (1956), chap. viii; Woodworth (1948), pp. 151–55.

ever, soon branched out into his own special areas of interest and developed his Field Theory. Like Koffka, he took the concept from physics of a dynamic *field,* like a magnetic field, where all the particles interact with each other and each particle is therefore subject to forces determined by patterns in the field at a particular moment. He concentrated his research on *motivation* of human behavior, which he conceived of as energy related to psychological *tension systems.*

His most important concept was that of the *life space* within which behavior takes place. The individual's life space is more than his environment: it includes himself (with his fundamental needs and his particular momentary needs and intentions) and his "behavioral environment" (i.e., his environment, physical, social, and conceptual, as he perceives it in relation to his needs and intentions). The state of any part of this field (e.g., himself) depends on the state and interrelationships of any other part of the field at that particular moment. This life-space is viewed objectively by the observer, not through introspective reports, and so the approach from this point of view is behavioristic. Within this life-space there are *goals and goal-objects* related to needs of the individual which exert an attractive force or a repellent force (i.e., which have a *positive* or a *negative valence*) and produce tension systems which determine the locomotion or movement of the individual within the life-space. Tension systems are, according to Lewin, basic to any motor behavior or activity. A person may be attracted to a particular goal (this attraction being perceived by him in the present state of his needs) but find a *barrier* separating him from the goal. This barrier is frustrating and arouses tensions which lead to various effects according to the state of the field. A tension may be aroused which will not be reduced until an alternative route has been found to the goal; another goal may exert a stronger attraction in view of the barrier; or the barrier may be so frustrating that the individual "leaves the field" or gives up the attempt to reach the goal, temporarily or finally. Lewin has studied various combinations of goals and barriers in both individual and group situations. He has also studied the selection of goals and the meaning of rewards for the individual in relation to his *ego-involvement* (the degree to which the goals are real to him) and his *level of aspiration* (his momentary goals).

Lewin worked out a mathematical correlate of his system, using topology and vector analysis, and so attempted to quantify his theories. It is not necessary, however, to have a profound knowledge of mathematics to draw a great deal of value from his research, much of which was in the area of social psychology. With relation to reinforcement and the Law of Effect, he drew attention to many features of the "behavioral environment" and the social environment which determine what will be rewarding and what will be punishing (or what will signify success or failure) to the individual. He also studied the connection between aroused tension systems and memory. His system has been productive of much research which is continuing.

OSGOOD AND MEDIATION THEORY[15]

We have already seen how Hull made considerable use of intervening variables, such as fractional, antedating goal responses, in his systematic theory. More and more psychologists have felt the necessity for positing some mediating processes between observed stimulus and response to explain such things as the effect of reinforcement in drive reduction, when primary drive reduction (e.g., satiation of hunger) comes some time after the administering of the reinforcement with many other events intervening. Also in need of explanation is the persistent effect of stimuli from previous experiences, as in simple conditioning or instrumental conditioning. When an animal acts in a certain way to avoid a painful stimulus on hearing a buzzer which has previously preceded this painful stimulus, what elements are involved in this "foresight," or, as Hull put it, in reacting "to the not-here and the not-now"?

Neobehaviorists are interested in *inferred mediating processes* and refer to them in terms of stimulus and response. Osgood, for instance, proposes a $S-r_m-s_m-R$ formula,

---

[15] Osgood (1953), (1962).

where r_m and s_m are mediating response and self-stimulus within the organism. According to this formula, a stimulus (S) has a number of environmental stimuli associated with it which impinge on the organism simultaneously. These become conditioned to the complex of reactions which the object itself arouses. When they appear later, independent of the original stimulus-object, they continue to elicit part of the total reaction to that object and thus become *signs* of that object. Some part of this reaction to the sign becomes a stable mediation process. When these *mediating reactions* (r_m) are aroused, they cause self-stimulation (s_m) which sets in motion certain instrumental sequences of responses (R). These mediating reactions may be aroused by the object itself or, in its absence, by stimuli associated with the object. In the latter case, they may arouse behavior which would have been directed to the object had it been present (e.g., anxiety or avoidance behavior). The same formula is used by Osgood to explain *"meaning"* in language usage, the word as sign arousing some part of the total re-action which would have been aroused by the object or event itself.

This formula is capable of much elaboration to cover the occurrence in the absence of a stimulus of many forms of behavior associated with that stimulus, behavior reappearing after a long interval, effects of delayed reinforcement, etc. Its use in the area of "meaning" in language is discussed at length in chapter xii.

MOWRER'S REVISED TWO-FACTOR THEORY[16]

Other neobehaviorists have been interested in fear or anxiety as an intervening variable. We have already discussed this in connection with the work of N. Miller, with whom O. H. Mowrer worked in close association at one time. Mowrer's ideas have passed through several stages, and finally he has become convinced that conditioning of the emotions of hope and fear is central in the learning process. His latest formulation, which he calls his *Revised Two-Factor Theory*, is an attempt to demonstrate that Pavlovian

---

[16] Mowrer (1960*a*), (1960*b*).

or classical conditioning and Thorndikean trial-and-error learning are fundamentally a single type, which he calls *sign learning,* the organism learning to react to signals or signs as well as to the things signalized. Even instrumental learning, according to Mowrer, is sign learning, and *extinction* is a reversal of the meaning of signs. To understand Mowrer's use of the word "sign" in this context, we may refer back to the explanation of a sign in Osgood's system. By *stimulus substitution,* stimuli which appear in association with the natural stimulus are conditioned to the same mediating reaction and so become "signs" of the original stimulus-object. When they reappear they arouse the same mediating reaction as if the stimulus-object were present, although often in attenuated form. Words may be signs for stimulus-objects in this way (see diagram in chapter xii).

With this as a background, we may move on to Mowrer's distinctive theory. According to Mowrer, it is *emotions* which are conditionable, not behavior, and so any conditioned response is an emotional response (part of the mediating reaction) which acts as a drive exciting the individual to action. The emotions of fear and hope, and their counterparts relief and disappointment, are intervening variables or mediating reactions which become conditioned to stimuli inherently associated with some action which brings reward or punishment, and it is these mediating reactions which constitute the *habit,* not the specific behavior which they produce.

Reinforcement

Mowrer's theory is two-factored because he postulates two types of reinforcement: incremental reinforcement or secondary punishment (where the emotion of fear or disappointment is aroused), and decremental reinforcement or reward (where the drive of fear is reduced and hope or relief is aroused).

In *incremental reinforcement,* or a punishment situation, *fear* is aroused by a sign which indicates the imminent onset of a painful stimulus, or *disappointment* is aroused by the withdrawal of a hope-arousing sign before its confirmation.

These emotions have previously been conditioned to extrinsic, *environmental stimuli* or to *response-correlated stimuli*, stimuli of a visual, kinesthetic, tactile, or proprioceptive character which form part of the sensation experienced when we act. When the fear drives us to action, there is a *positive* (attractive) or *negative* (repellent) *feedback* from such stimulation. With incremental reinforcement or secondary punishment, the fear may act as a drive to action, if the stimulus is external, and cause *active avoidance behavior*, an impulse to get away from the situation. Response-correlated stimulation, or negative feedback, on the other hand, may cause conflict when the fear drive is active, and this will inhibit action and cause *passive avoidance behavior*, an impulse to remain inactive and keep away from the unpleasant situation.

In a *decremental reinforcement* or reward situation, *relief* is experienced at a sign that an impending objectionable event has been averted (in this case, there is fear-reduction), or *hope* is aroused by a sign which indicates the imminent occurrence of some desired event. These emotions have been conditioned previously to environmental or response-correlated stimuli. Both relief and hope are reinforcing, and constitute two types of *secondary reinforcement*. Once again, it is the mediating reaction, represented by these emotions, which constitutes the *habit*, and not a physical response. This fear reduction may be satisfying, or a reinforcing hopefulness may lead to excitement and heightened activity, as informational feedback from the environment and from the response-correlated stimuli is positive. The latter results in active approach behavior leading to consummatory action.

As it is the *mediating reaction* which is conditioned and constitutes the habit, extinction of physical responses is not simply a matter of these responses being unrewarded, but is due to the extinguishing of the hope reaction, which in Mowrer's system is secondary reinforcement. There is therefore a change in the significance of signs, the environmental and response-correlated stimuli aroused by the sign no longer arousing hope. When at a later stage the sign comes to have the same meaning for the individual as be-

fore, these physical responses will reappear. So Mowrer
maintains that it is the relative attractiveness of a response
that is altered by learning, and not the physical response
itself.

The Symbolic Processes

Mowrer has taken a special interest in the problems
associated with human "symbolic processes" (concept formation, meaning, the acquisition of language, thinking)
and he examines these from the point of view of mediating
reactions.

Going right back to the acquisition of the native language
by the infant, Mowrer finds the role of emotion fundamental here as well. His experiments with talking birds and his
observations with children have led him to an *autism* or
self-satisfaction theory of native-language learning. He
believes that the child feels warm affection for his mother
from whom he first hears words. He then repeats over and
over what he has heard because the words recreate for him
the presence of the loved person. This provides self-ad-
ministered reinforcement of the language behavior, secondary reinforcement having become attached to the
response-correlated stimuli. The words learned in this way
are found to be instrumentally effective in obtaining for
the child what he wants, thus providing him with primary
reinforcement. They then become an established part of his
repertoire.

Mowrer's formula for the acquisition of *word-meanings*
is similar to Osgood's: the word is originally experienced
in association with an object or situation which is itself
meaningful, and part of this total reaction is conditioned
as a mediating reaction. This part of the total reaction is
the "meaning" of the word for the individual and will be
aroused later by the word itself. In *The Measurement of
Meaning*, Osgood and his colleagues have shown that there
is a strong element in meaning that is emotional and evaluative (see chapter xii). Mowrer speaks of this element as
an image of "value," "images" being conditioned sensations. The cognitive or denotative element he calls an
image of "fact." The proportion of "meaning" which is

cognitive and the proportion which is evaluative will vary from individual to individual. In a social group, there will be a certain stability of meaning for most words because of common experiences, but there will still be a certain part of this distinctive mediating reaction which will be derived from the particular experiences of the individual. Thus "grape" can "mean" pleasant sensations for one child but can arouse an unpleasant reaction in a child who has just recovered from the painful effects of eating unripe grapes.

"Meanings" for words may also be acquired from their association with other words, and this "meaning" may then generalize to the object when it appears, affecting the attitude toward that object. In this way children can be made to fear objects which formerly did not frighten them.

Meaning, for Mowrer, fits into the general pattern of incremental and decremental reinforcement which is the core of his theory. If mere contiguity were all that was involved in word acquisition, without these elements of secondary motivation and secondary reinforcement (fear and hope), the organism would form many useless associations, and it would be difficult to explain many facts in the development of an individual vocabulary and specific personal reactions by a person living in a social community.

The mediation approach to meaning easily accommodates the observed fact that different words can arouse very similar responses (synonyms). This happens because they are conditioned to the same mediating reaction. The process is called *mediated equivalence of cues*. On the other hand, objects or situations which appear very similar to others are distinguished for the individual by the mediated meaning they have acquired for him. This process is called *mediated discrimination of cues*.

An understanding of the part played by this mediating reaction in meaning clarifies what Mowrer intends to convey when he says that in communication we are transferring meanings from sign to sign within another person.[17] We do not transfer meanings to that person, but by asso-

---

[17] Mowrer (1960b), p. 139.

ciating and combining the meanings he already possesses in new ways we give information. This is why there is so much misunderstanding even among people who speak the same language, and why discussion often begins with a clarification of the meanings certain signs have for the persons speaking. Even this does not insure perfect comprehension, as other signs are being used in the explanation of signs, and these too have acquired personal "meaning."

Mowrer's mediation theory accounts not only for meaning but also for thought, in the sense of "intricate and elaborate processes intervening between the end results of learning and the execution of behavior."[18] These processes make for the infinite variety and frequent unpredictability of behavior. Mowrer maintains that emotions are the "core of thought in that they *mediate* between primary drives and the real consequences of various possible actions," thus guiding the subsequent course of overt behavior.[19]

NEUROPSYCHOLOGY

K. Lashley[20] is a behaviorist who has devoted his life to neuropsychology. He has studied the brain, trying to locate psychological functions and learning in specific parts of the cerebral cortex, but he has found that a certain number of functions can be learned by any part of the cortex and that most habits are dependent on mass action of the whole central nervous system. His research has led him to the decision that the brain is not simply a switchboard, transferring incoming nerve impulses to outgoing nerves. He is convinced that it has a more active role, and that behavior is more complicated than a conditioned reflex would lead one to believe.

The subject of thought in behavior has been the special study of *D. O. Hebb*,[21] who is also a neuropsychologist. He bases his theory on what is known of the structure of the brain, moving from physical facts to inferences about its

---

[18] *Ibid.*, p. 211.
[19] *Ibid.*, p. 217.
[20] Woodworth (1948), pp. 98–103.
[21] Hebb (1949), (1953).

possible functioning. Hebb believes that the brain has an intrinsic organization of cortical activity, as shown by the slow waves of an infant's electroencephalogram, and that when sensory impressions impinge upon it they form through repeated impressions what he calls *cell assemblies*. When such a sensory impression reappears, the cell assembly is fired. A whole series of cell assemblies may be aroused as a *phase sequence*, and this constitutes a thought process.

In an adult, these phase sequences are well developed and interconnected. There is a perceptual organization and a conceptual development with growth. Adult learning is not a matter of new associations between totally unrelated processes but is a strengthening of facilitations among cell assemblies and phase sequences which are already in activity, and therefore a changed relationship between the central effects of the separate stimulations. As these phase sequences and cell assemblies are originally fired by sensorily perceived environmental stimuli, even though this stimulation continues within the brain cells without further external stimulation, the control really comes back to the environment and so the theory is not animistic. It is this continued stimulation within the brain cells which allows time for the development of permanent associations. In view of the elaborate interconnections of cell assemblies, Hebb has suggested that the train of thought may not be a single series but may exist in multiple parallel.

Hebb's cell assemblies with their interassociations are not unlike the mediating reactions posited by Osgood which may be aroused by a number of different stimuli or may activate a number of different behavioral responses. Hebb speaks of a central core of conceptual activity which dominates in arousing a system as a whole but which has a fringe content of "meaning" which may vary with the circumstances of arousal.

THE CYBERNETIC MODEL[22]

Application of the principles of control systems in machines to human behavior patterns has aroused consider-

---

[22] Hilgard (1958), pp. 376–77; Mowrer (1960*b*), chap. vii.

able interest in recent years. The central concept is that of
"feedback." Just as a thermostat registers the results of its
operation, compares these with the original instructions,
and adapts its operation accordingly, so in many phases of
human activity the organism seems to adapt its performance according to "feedback" or information on the results of its previous performance. Negative feedback, indicating the degree to which performance deviates from the
desired behavior, leads to corrective adaptations. Mowrer
and others have shown the importance of feedback in human speech by their experiments with delayed, auditory
feedback, and feedback is implied in the term "response-
correlated stimuli." The feedback model helps to explain
some of the apparently teleological features of the Law of
Effect where an action appears to be influenced by its consequences, in that results will increase or decrease the like-
lihood of its recurrence. Some psychologists believe that
there is constant activity in the nervous system and that
feedback makes possible a continuous readaptation and correction of maladaptive responses, even while they are occurring.

G. A. *Miller*[23] has taken special interest in psychological
problems associated with language and the process of communication. He has familiarized himself with the field of
structural linguistics and has worked closely in some of his
research with Noam Chomsky. This special interest in language has led him into the areas of verbal learning and
verbal habits (experiments with rote learning and recall
of nonsense syllables and meaningful materials, word association tests, verbal context, and redundancy), of acous-
tics as related to the problems of producing and perceiving
speech, of information theory as used by communications
engineers (see chapter x), and of cybernetics, or the study
of control processes in machines.

Much research into human thought processes has been
conducted by communications and electronic computer engineers, and Miller and his associates have used the model
of the computer Plan (or program) to illustrate the work-

---

[23] G. Miller (1950) ; Miller, Galanter, and Pribram (1960).

ings of human behavior, and so have moved to a mediation position. One of the major problems facing the psychological theorist is a comprehensive explanation of how incoming impulses are translated into outgoing impulses in human behavior, and it is to this problem that Miller's hypothesis is addressed. He and his associates suggest that behavior is organized at several levels of complexity, higher-level Plans setting lower-level Plans in operation, the higher-level Plan representing the strategy and the lower-level Plan the tactics. These Plans result from the organized knowledge which the organism has accumulated about itself and the world. The model is worked out in considerable detail in *Plans and the Structure of Behavior* by Miller and associates.

THE FUNCTIONALISTS[24]

A very old school of psychology which has not been mentioned so far is functionalism. Perhaps it has been left for last because its approach is eclectic (Woodworth calls it "the middle of the road") and its tenets are experimental rather than theoretical.

The functionalist asks how and why, as well as what (as Angell expressed it), seeking the functional relationships between variables in the study of human behavior. He is not wedded to any hard-and-fast theoretical position, although he may have a leaning toward associationism. He is dedicated to the method of experimental science: of testing hypotheses by systematically varying conditions and examining the function of each variable. He also seeks to understand physiological components of behavior and thought-processes, which he penetrates by the method of introspection (with careful safeguards and controls). He draws on the findings and vocabulary of various theoretical positions, always experimenting to fill in the gaps and explain the difficult cases which do not fit into other people's theories. He designs experiments with animals and with human subjects and is particularly inclined to research which has some practical use and application. Functionalists have carried

---

[24] Woodworth (1948), chaps. ii and viii; Hilgard (1956), chap. x.

out much valuable experimental research on problems of human learning: on motivation; the importance of set and attitudes; sensory perception; how the organism first discovers an adequate response, and what conditions tend to establish or eliminate this response; factors at work in rate of learning, transfer, and retention; and the effects of distribution of practice and of meaningfulness of materials for learning. Functionalists whose work has been quoted in this book include Woodworth, McGeoch, Irion, Hilgard, Melton, McClelland, and Underwood.

SELECTED READINGS

HILGARD, E. R. *Theories of Learning.* 2d ed. New York: Appleton-Century-Crofts, Inc., 1956. Pp. 563. A standard reference work which gives a full account of nine established theories, with supporting experimental evidence and bibliographic information. It also describes fully the latest trends in experimentation and the outstanding issues that are still unresolved. It requires study and concentration.

KELLER, F., and SCHOENFELD, W. *Principles of Psychology.* New York: Appleton-Century-Crofts, Inc., 1950. Pp. 431. A very readable account of behaviorist principles and experimentation. Designed for beginning psychology students, it explains the terminology and positions taken very simply.

McGEOCH, J., and IRION, A. *The Psychology of Human Learning.* New York: Longmans, Green & Co., 1952. Pp. 596. Concentrates on those parts of the experimental literature which contribute directly to an understanding of human learning, taking as chapter headings areas of learning rather than theoretical positions.

OSGOOD, C. E. *Method and Theory in Experimental Psychology.* New York: Oxford University Press, 1953. Pp. 800. Covers the field of experimental literature from the point of view of critical theoretical issues. It endeavors to bridge the gap between behaviorism and Gestalt psychology with a mediation theory, and gives full details of experiments with interpretative comment.

SAPORTA, S. (ed.). *Psycholinguistics, a Book of Readings.* New York: Holt, Rinehart, & Winston, 1961. Pp. 551.

Draws together the most significant articles on language by linguists and behavioral psychologists in the last twenty-five years.

WOODWORTH, R. S. *Contemporary Schools of Psychology.* Rev. ed. New York: Ronald Press Co., 1948. Pp. 279. A short, readable account of the development of psychology as an experimental science and the viewpoints and personalities associated with the principal schools. This book is an excellent introduction for readers with no knowledge of the subject.

WOODWORTH, R. S., and SCHLOSBERG, H. *Experimental Psychology.* Rev. ed. New York: Holt, Rinehart & Winston, 1954. Pp. 948. A detailed survey of the experimental data from an eclectic point of view. It is very well indexed, and material on an area of special interest is easy to find.

Reference material on individual psychologists can be found in the general bibliography under the name of the psychologist.

BIBLIOGRAPHY

AGARD, F., and DUNKEL, H. 1948. *An Investigation of Second-Language Teaching*. Boston: Ginn & Co.

ALLEN, HAROLD B. (ed.). 1958. *Readings in Applied English Linguistics*. New York: Appleton-Century-Crofts, Inc.

ANDERSSON, T. 1961. "After FLES—What?" *Educational Forum*, XXVI (November, 1961), 81.

ANSHEN, RUTH (ed.). 1957. *Language: An Enquiry into Its Meaning and Function*. New York: Harper & Bros.

AUDIO-LINGUAL MATERIALS (A-L M). 1961. *Teacher's Manual, French, Level One*. New York: Harcourt, Brace & World, Inc.

BIRKMAIER, E. M. 1958. "Foreign Languages—Review of the Literature," *Review of Educational Research* (April, 1958).

BLAIR, G.; JONES, R.; and SIMPSON, R. 1962. *Educational Psychology*. 2d ed. New York: Macmillan Co.

BROOKS, NELSON. 1960. *Language and Language Learning —Theory and Practice*. New York: Harcourt, Brace & World, Inc.

BROWN, ROGER. 1958. *Words and Things*. Glencoe, Ill.: Free Press.

BRUNO, J. R., and SIMCHES, S. O. 1962. "A Psycholinguistic Rationale for FLES," *French Review*, XXXV, No. 6 (May, 1962).

CARMICHAEL, L. (ed.). 1946. *Manual of Child Psychology*. New York: John Wiley & Sons.

CARROLL, JOHN B. 1953. *The Study of Language*. Cambridge, Mass.: Harvard University Press.

———. 1963. "Research on Teaching Foreign Languages," in *Handbook of Research on Teaching*, ed. N. Gage (Chicago: Rand McNally & Co.).

CHOMSKY, NOAM. 1959. Review of B. F. Skinner's *Verbal Behavior*, in *Language*. XXXV (January-March, 1959).

CONANT, JAMES B. 1959. *The American High School Today: A First Report to Interested Citizens*. New York: McGraw-Hill Book Co.

CURRAN, CHARLES A. 1961. "Counseling Skills Adapted to the Learning of Foreign Languages," *Bulletin of the Menninger Clinic*, XXV, No. 2 (March, 1961).

DOLLARD, JOHN, and MILLER, NEAL. 1950. *Personality and Psychotherapy: An Analysis in Terms of Learning, Thinking and Culture*. New York: McGraw-Hill Book Co.

DUNKEL, H. B. 1948. *Second-Language Learning*. Boston: Ginn & Co.

DUNKEL, H., and PILLET, R. 1962. *French in the Elementary School: Five Years' Experience*. Chicago: University of Chicago Press.

FLAXMAN, SEYMOUR L. (ed.). 1961. *Modern Language Teaching in School and College*. Northeast Conference on the Teaching of Foreign Languages, 1961: Reports of the Working Committees. Princeton, N.J.: Princeton University Press.

FRIES, CHARLES C. 1954. "Meaning and Linguistic Analysis." *Language*, XXX (January-March, 1954), 57–68. Reprinted in HAROLD B. ALLEN (ed.), *Readings in Applied English Linguistics* (1958), pp. 101–13.

———. 1945. *Teaching and Learning English as a Foreign Language*. Ann Arbor: University of Michigan Press.

GAGNE, ROBERT M. 1962. "Military Training and Principles of Learning," *American Psychologist*, XVII (February, 1962).

GEORGETOWN UNIVERSITY, SCHOOL OF FOREIGN SERVICE. 1955. *Report of the Sixth Annual Round Table Meeting on Linguistics and Language Teaching*. Washington, D. C.: Georgetown University Press.

GESELL, ARNOLD. 1940. *The First Five Years of Life: A Guide to the Study of the Preschool Child*. New York: Harper & Bros.

GLEASON, H. A. 1961. *An Introduction to Descriptive Linguistics*. Rev. ed. New York: Holt, Rinehart & Winston, Inc.

HALL, EDWARD T. 1959. *The Silent Language*. New York: Doubleday & Co.

HAMP, ERIC P. 1957. *A Glossary of American Technical Linguistic Usage 1925–1950*. Utrecht and Antwerp: Spectrum Publishers.

HEBB, D. O. 1949. *The Organization of Behavior: A Neuropsychological Theory*. New York: John Wiley and Sons, 1949.

———. 1953. "On Human Thought," *Canadian Journal of Psychology*, VII (1953), 99–110.

HECHINGER, FRED M. 1963. "Foreign Languages Stage a Comeback," *Saturday Review*, February 16, 1963.

HILGARD, E. R. 1956. *Theories of Learning*, 2d ed. New York: Appleton-Century-Crofts, Inc.

HILL, ARCHIBALD A. 1958. *Introduction to Linguistic Structures*. New York: Harcourt, Brace & Co.

HJELMSLEV, LOUIS. 1961. *Prolegomena to a Theory of Language*. Translated by FRANCIS J. WHITFIELD. Madison: University of Wisconsin Press.

HOBBS, NICHOLAS. 1953. "Child Development and Language Learning," *School and Society*, LXXVIII (1953), No. 2012.

HOCKETT, C. 1958. *A Course in Modern Linguistics*. New York: Macmillan Co.

HOIJER, HARRY (ed.). 1954. *Language in Culture*. American Anthropological Association Memoir, No. 79, Vol. LVI, No. 6 (December, 1954). Also published by the University of Chicago Press (1954).

HOLTON, J.; KING, P.; MATHIEU, G.; and POND, K. 1961. *Sound Language Teaching. The State of the Art Today*. New York: University Publishers.

HUSE, H. R. 1931. *The Psychology of Foreign Language Study*. Chapel Hill: University of North Carolina Press.

HUTCHINSON, JOSEPH C. 1961. *Modern Foreign Languages in High School: The Language Laboratory*. Washington, D. C.: U. S. Dept. of Education.

INHELDER, BARBEL, and PIAGET, JEAN. 1958. Translated by A. PARSONS and S. MILGRAM, *The Growth of Logical Thinking from Childhood to Adolescence*. New York: Basic Books, Inc.

JONES, M. R. (ed.). 1960. *Nebraska Symposium on Motivation.* Lincoln: University of Nebraska Press.

JOOS, M. (ed.). 1958. *Readings in Linguistics.* New York: American Council of Learned Societies.

KATONA, GEORGE. 1940. *Organizing and Memorizing—Studies in the Psychology of Learning and Teaching.* New York: Columbia University Press.

KEATING, RAYMOND. 1963. *A Study of the Effectiveness of Language Laboratories.* New York: Institute of Administrative Research, Teachers College, Columbia University.

KELLER, FRED, and SCHOENFELD, WILLIAM. 1950. *Principles of Psychology.* New York: Appleton-Century-Crofts, Inc.

LAMBERT, WALLACE. 1961. *A Study of the Roles of Attitudes and Motivation in Second Language Learning.* N.D.E.A. Project Report, SAE-8817. Montreal, Canada.

———. 1963. "Psychological Approaches to the Study of Language." Part I: "On Learning, Thinking and Human Abilities," *Modern Language Journal,* XLVII, No. 2, 51–62. Part II: "On Second-Language Learning and Bi-Lingualism," *ibid.,* XLVII, No. 3, 114–21.

LASHLEY, K. 1951. "The Problem of Serial Order in Behavior," in L. JEFFRESS (ed.). *Cerebral Mechanisms in Behavior: The Hixon Symposium.* New York: J. Wiley & Sons.

LEOPOLD, WERNER. 1949. *Speech Development of a Bilingual Child: A Linguist's Record.* 4 vols. Evanston, Ill.: Northwestern University Press.

LEWIS, M. M. 1936. *Infant Speech: A Study of the Beginnings of Language.* London: Kegan Paul, Trench, Trubner Co.

———. 1957. *How Children Learn to Speak.* London: G. Harrap Co.

LURIA, A. R. 1959. "The Directive Function of Speech in Development and Dissolution," *Word,* XV, No. 2 (August, 1959), 341–52; *ibid.,* XV, No. 3 (December, 1959), 453–64.

McGEOCH, JOHN, and IRION, ARTHUR. 1952. *The Psychology of Human Learning.* New York: Longmans, Green & Co.

MANDELBAUM, DAVID G. (ed.). 1958. *Selected Writings of*

Edward Sapir in Language, Culture and Personality. Berkeley: University of California Press.

MARTINET, ANDRE. 1953. "Structural Linguistics," in *Anthropology Today.* Chicago: University of Chicago Press.

MARTY, FERNAND. 1960. "Language Laboratory Learning," Wellesley, Mass.: Audio-Visual Publications.

————. 1963. *Linguistics Applied to the Beginning French Course.* Roanoke, Va.: Audio-Visual Publications.

MILLER, GEORGE A. 1951. *Language and Communication.* New York: McGraw-Hill Book Co.

MILLER, G. A.; GALANTER, E.; and PRIBRAM, KARL. 1960. *Plans and the Structure of Behavior.* New York: Henry Holt & Co.

MILLER, NEAL, and DOLLARD, JOHN. 1941. *Social Learning and Imitation.* New Haven, Conn.: Yale University Press.

MODERN LANGUAGE ASSOCIATION OF AMERICA. "Foreign-Language Program Policy," *PMLA,* September, 1956, Part II.

————. 1959–61. *Reports of Surveys and Studies in the Teaching of Modern Foreign Languages.* New York: Modern Language Association.

MOHRMANN, C.; SOMMERFELT, A.; and WHATMOUGH, J. (eds.). 1961. *Trends in European and American Linguistics, 1930–1960.* Utrecht: Spectrum Publishers.

MOWRER, O. HOBART. 1960a. *Learning Theory and Behavior.* New York: John Wiley & Sons.

————. 1960b. *Learning Theory and the Symbolic Processes.* New York: John Wiley & Sons.

NIDA, E. A. 1952. *God's Word in Man's Language.* New York: Harper & Bros.

————. 1957. "Motivation in Second Language Learning," *Language Learning,* VII (1956–57), Nos. 3 and 4, 11.

————. 1958. "Some Psychological Problems in Language Learning," *ibid.,* VIII (1957–58), Nos. 1 and 2, 7.

O'CONNOR, PATRICIA. 1961. *Modern Foreign Languages in High School: Pre-Reading Instruction.* Washington, D. C.: U. S. Office of Education.

OINAS, FELIX J. 1960. *Language Teaching Today.* Vol. XXVI, No. 4 of *International Journal of American Lin-*

guistics. Bloomington: Indiana University Research Center in Anthropology, Folklore and Linguistics.

OSGOOD, C. E. 1953. *Method and Theory in Experimental Psychology*. New York: Oxford University Press.

————. 1962. "Studies on the Generality of Affective Meaning Systems," *American Psychologist*, XVII (January, 1962).

OSGOOD, C.; SUCI, G.; and TANNENBAUM, P. 1957. *The Measurement of Meaning*. Urbana: University of Illinois Press.

PARKER, W. R. 1962. *The National Interest and Foreign Languages*. 3d ed. Washington, D. C.: U. S. Department of State.

PIMSLEUR, P. 1959. Report of the N.D.E.A. Conference on *Psychological Experiments Related to Second Language Learning*. Los Angeles: University of California.

————. 1961. *Under-Achievement in Foreign Language Learning*. N.D.E.A. Project OE-2-14-004, Report No. II. Columbus, Ohio.

PIMSLEUR, P.; MACE, L.; and KEISLAR, EVAN. 1961. *Preliminary Discrimination Training in the Teaching of French Pronunciation*. N.D.E.A. Project SAE 8950. Los Angeles: University of California.

POLITZER, R. L. 1961. *Teaching French: An Introduction to Applied Linguistics*. Boston: Ginn & Co.

————. 1961. *Teaching Spanish: A Linguistic Orientation*. Boston: Ginn & Co.

Proceedings of the VIII International Congress of Linguists. 1958. Oslo: Oslo University Press.

SAPORTA, SOL (ed.). 1961. *Psycholinguistics: A Book of Readings*. New York: Holt, Rinehart & Winston.

SAUSSURE, FERDINAND DE. 1959. *Course in General Linguistics*. Edited by C. BALLY and A. SECHEHAYE and translated by WADE BASKIN. New York: Philosophical Library, Inc.

SCHERER, GEORGE. 1961. Progress Report on *The German Teaching Experiment at the University of Colorado*, N.D.E.A.

SKINNER, B. F. 1948. *Verbal Behavior* ("William James

Lectures.") Cambridge, Mass.: Harvard University Press.

———. 1957. *Verbal Behavior.* New York: Appleton-Century-Crofts, Inc.

SPENCE, K. W. 1956. *Behavior Theory and Conditioning.* New Haven, Conn.: Yale University Press.

STACK, EDWARD. 1960. *The Language Laboratory and Modern Language Teaching.* New York: Oxford University Press.

STARR, W.; THOMPSON, M. P.; and WALSH, D. (eds.). 1960. *Modern Foreign Languages and the Academically Talented Student.* New York: National Education Association and Modern Language Association of America.

STEVENS, S. S. (ed.). 1951. *Handbook of Experimental Psychology.* New York: John Wiley & Sons.

SUPPES, P. and WEIR, R. 1961. Progress Reports 1 and 2 of the *Project for Application of Learning Theory to Problems of Second Language Acquisition.* N.D.E.A. Stanford, Calif.: Stanford University.

Teacher's Manual, prepared by the staff of the Modern Language Materials Development Center (New York, 1961). See AUDIO-LINGUAL MATERIALS. 1961.

TIKHOMIROV, O. K. 1959. Review of B. F. SKINNER'S *Verbal Behavior. Word,* XV, No. 2 (August, 1959), 362–67.

Trends in European and American Linguistics, 1930–1960. See MOHRMANN, C.; SOMMERFELT, A.; and WHATMOUGH, J. (eds.). 1961.

TUFTS UNIVERSITY. 1961. *Interdisciplinary Research Seminar on Psycholinguistics and Foreign Language Teaching.* SAE-9494.

UNDERWOOD, BENTON J. 1949. *Experimental Psychology: An Introduction.* New York: Appleton-Century-Crofts, Inc.

UNDERWOOD, B. J., and SCHULZ, R. W. 1960. *Meaningfulness and Verbal Learning.* Chicago: J. B. Lippincott & Co.

UNESCO. 1955. *The Teaching of Modern Languages.* Paris: UNESCO.

U. S. DEPT. OF EDUCATION, N.D.E.A. LANGUAGE DEVELOPMENT PROGRAM. 1961. *Research and Studies, Report on the*

First Two Years, OE-12011, and *Second Report*, OE-12011-61.

————. 1963. *Completed Research, Studies and Instructional Materials, List No. 2* (OE 12016). *Research and Studies Contracted in Fiscal Year 1962* (OE-12014-62). Washington, D. C.: U. S. Government Printing Office.

VALDMAN, A. 1960. "From Structural Analysis to Pattern Drill," *French Review*, XXXIV, No. 2 (December, 1960), 170–81.

WERTHEIMER, M. 1945. *Productive Thinking*. New York: Harper & Bros.

WIENER, NORBERT. 1954. *The Human Use of Human Beings: Cybernetics and Society*. New York: Doubleday & Co. (Anchor Books).

WOODWORTH, ROBERT S. 1948. *Contemporary Schools of Psychology*. Rev. ed. New York: Ronald Press Co.

————. 1958. *Dynamics of Behavior*. New York: Henry Holt Co.

WOODWORTH, R., and SCHLOSBERG, H. 1954. *Experimental Psychology*. Rev. ed. New York: Holt, Rinehart, & Winston, Inc.

INDEX

Abilities, 94, 95, 179
Abstraction, 75, 173
Acquired cue value; *see* Cues, acquired value of stimuli as
Acquired drive; *see* Drive, acquired
Affect, 98
Agard-Dunkel investigation, 58, 73, 86
A-L M[aterials], 12, 36, 41
American students; *see* Students, American
Analogy, 21–22, 102, 115–30, 152, 153
Analysis, 21–22, 115–30, 153, 157; *see also* Linguistic analysis.
Anderson, T., 2
Angell, J. R., 191
Animal experiments, 191; Köhler, 180; Pavlov, 165, 166–68; Mowrer, 186; Skinner, 52, 176; Spence, 55; Tolman, 57
Anshen, Ruth, 23
Anticipatory response; *see* Response, anticipatory
Anxiety, 37, 48, 84, 86, 92, 93, 97, 104, 106, 128, 183; as a drive, 49, 54, 55, 82, 171
Approval, 54, 69, 86, 91, 93, 156, 157
Aspiration, level of, 59–60, 69, 162, 182
Assigns (Osgood), 145
Association, 19, 31, 43, 52, 63, 66, 92, 98, 106, 107, 108, 110–12, 113, 123, 125, 138, 142, 143, 144, 145, 149, 150, 154, 156, 160, 166, 171, 177, 186, 187, 189
Associationists, 165, 191
Associative shifting, 39, 166

Attitude; *see* Set
Attraction; *see* Cathexis
Audio-lingual materials, 7, 42, 69, 99; *see also* A-L M[aterials]
Audio-lingual method, 7, 8, 10–18, 29, 33, 43, 58, 62, 64, 66, 67, 73, 83, 84, 87, 95, 100, 102, 109, 113, 114, 115, 118, 119, 120, 121, 142, 143, 145, 146, 149, 151, 154, 156, 159; assumptions of the, 8, 19–22
Audio-lingual stage, 21, 94, 100, 112
Auditory discrimination, 37, 53, 58, 93, 96, 106, 108, 109, 110, 112, 160
Aural comprehension; *see* Listening comprehension
Aural-oral method, 19, 43, 78, 86, 100
Autism theory of language learning, 29, 186
Automatic response, 15–17, 19, 30, 31, 40, 41, 47, 73, 75, 101, 116–17, 120, 129, 149, 151, 152, 153, 156, 162
Aversion, 92, 160
Avoidance behavior; *see* Behavior, avoidance

Barrier, 94, 172, 181
Bartley, S. H., and Chute, E., 70
Behavior, 136; animal, 168; approach, 185; avoidance, 37, 128, 150, 182, 183, 185; copying, 48, 49, 50; fixated, 93; in the foreign language, 94, 116; human, 22, 57, 73, 135, 147, 168, 173, 177, 179, 181, 188, 189, 191; matched-dependent, 48–50, 62, 63, 125; molar, 170, 171; molec-